North·South Center
UNIVERSITY OF MIAMI

I0127685

Cuba, Cubans and Cuban-Americans, 1902-1991:
A Bibliography

Jesse J. Dossick

Routledge
Taylor & Francis Group

LONDON AND NEW YORK

Research Institute
for Cuban Studies

THE NORTH-SOUTH CENTER promotes, through cultural and technical exchange, better relations among the United States, Canada, and the nations of Latin America and the Caribbean. The Center provides a disciplined, intellectual focus for improved relations, commerce, and understanding between North America and Latin America. The Center conducts programs of education, training, cooperative study, public outreach, and research and engages in an active program of publication and dissemination of information on the Americas. The North-South Center fosters linkages among academic and research institutions throughout the Americas and acts as an agent of change in the region.

First published 1992 by the University of Miami North-South Center

Published 2017 by Routledge
2 Park Square, Milton Park, Abingdon, Oxon OX14 4RN
711 Third Avenue, New York, NY 10017, USA

Routledge is an imprint of the Taylor & Francis Group, an informa business

ISBN 13: 978-0-935501-49-0 (pbk)

For Bea

Contents

INTRODUCTION

Fidel Castro's domination of Cuba since 1959, his cruel record in human rights, his aid to leftist governments and revolutionary movements in the Third World, the migration of thousands of Cuban citizens to mainland U.S.A., and the impact they have made upon the states, politically, economically, and socially, have contributed to a North American policy that strongly opposes relations with Castro and Cuba.

In the face of the dramatic developments in Eastern Europe and the *glasnost* policy of Soviet Union President Mikhail Gorbachev, one would like to assume that after a period of further economic stagnation hastened by cutbacks in Soviet subsidies and a reappraisal of trade arrangements with his Marxist partners in the Eastern bloc and Castro's desire to rejoin the Organization of American States, he might, despite his public utterances and actions to the contrary, slowly relinquish his strong support of Marxist principles and begin to ease up on his rigid stance vis-á-vis his domestic scene and relations with the United States. The question might arise then, what should our reaction and policy be if the change were to occur? While no public discussion on this possibility is on the horizon, undoubtedly within government and academic circles, reviews are under way, and options surely are being contemplated. For example, there must have been some consideration given to this possibility at the recent international conference of scholars concerned with Cuba held in Halifax, Nova Scotia the first week of November 1989 as well among the hundreds of Latin American experts attending the Conference of the Latin American Studies Association held in Miami during the first week of December 1989, and locally, during July 1991, Governor Lawton Chiles revived a Commission investigating the impact on Florida of an end to Castro's reign in Cuba.

For scholars and officials, it would be desirable and helpful to widen their knowledge of *all* aspects of Cuban life over and above the political which has dominated our policy, actions, books, periodicals, and press. It also would be helpful for the general public and for second- and third-generation Cuban Americans to learn more about that nation's art, anthropology, economy, education, history, music, dance, cinema, literature, other areas of Cuban life and culture that are not too well-known, and what has been researched about Cuban Americans here in the United States.

This void in our knowledge of Cuba can be rectified by calling attention to a rich source of information in doctoral dissertations, almost all of which has not been published. Although some dissertations find their way into public print as books, primarily with the aid of university presses, too many of them are only recorded partially as articles in periodicals or are inconspicuously shelved in university libraries. Two reasons for this situation are the high cost of publishing scholarly works with prospects of limited sales and that generally little attention is given to them other than through a listing such as this.

This classified bibliography of 900 dissertations accepted by North American, British, and Canadian universities is valuable for many other reasons. Scholars, specialists, and policy makers in various governmental agencies may learn of the availability of data heretofore unknown to them. Professors can take advantage of additional data to enrich lectures and, in their capacity as doctoral advisers, may find the list helpful in discussing the selection of research problems with doctoral candidates.

Unnecessary duplication will be avoided. Examination of the overall list will reveal where too much, and too little, research has been done. With the passing of years, earlier studies can be re-examined, added to, or the findings challenged with the presentation of new data.

The first doctoral dissertation dealing with Cuba, "The Relations of the United States and Cuba to 1830," was accepted at Harvard University in 1902, written by Francis Samuel Philbrick. In 1905, Hubert Aimes wrote "A History of Slavery in Cuba, 1511 to 1868." Since then another 892 dissertations have been accepted by 123 North American universities, 11 universities in great Britain, and eight universities in Canada. Incidentally, during the process of gathering the data for this list, the author came across six dissertations from the National University of Mexico (1982), the University of Havana (1949), the University of Paris (1905, 1934), Montpelier (1906), and

Geneva (1989). These have been included on the grounds that they may be useful to future researchers.

Prior to 1960, only 94 dissertations were accepted, with almost half that number being produced in the fifties alone. The vast bulk accepted in the 30 odd years since then reflects the growth in doctoral research as well as the great interest in Cuba, Cubans, and Cuban Americans.

New York University leads in output with Columbia and the University of Florida at very close seconds. The Universities of Texas, California at Berkeley, Miami, Yale, Harvard, and Florida State rank as the next large group of producers of Cuban studies. Half of the total number of universities listed produced three or less dissertations each: 30 produced only one, 16 produced only two, and 13 produced only three. Of the 16 dissertations credited to the 11 universities from Great Britain, London (7) and Oxford (7) produced more than half. The eight Canadian universities produced a total of eleven dissertations only, 10 of which were accepted in the seventies and eighties, dealing for the most part with political matters.

The great bulk of doctoral dissertations on Cuba was produced in literature (over 300) and proved to be a rich descriptive source of Cuban literature in general, with its history, folklore, and studies in profusion of three score individual writers and poets, down to two studies of literature of Cubans in exile. The history of Cuba is covered on a large scale with over 120 titles, classified by era, with only 11 studies examining different phases of Cuban history after 1959. This is compensated, however, with a total of 173 titles dealing with politics, the military, diplomacy, and foreign relations, almost all of which were written after 1959, with a major emphasis on U.S.-Cuban relations.

The classification on education contains 65 titles, 11 of which deal with Cuba, mostly Cuban history of education, with the remaining 51 studies of education of Cuban-Americans in the United States. Of the 60 dissertations found in sociology and cultural anthropology, 15 are concerned with Cuba per se and 45 with Cuban Americans in the United States.

Generally, in the economics classification (39 titles) most of which was produced in the sixties and seventies, the Cuban economy under Castro (12 dissertations with only three since 1978) was studied very little because of our limited opportunities to gain access to data and to study it from the mainland.

The section on psychology (23 titles), has only one study of schizophrenia in Havana, and the remaining 22 studies deal with the psychological problems of Cuban Americans.

Apart from one dissertation in political geography dealing with Cuba in part (1981), no other doctoral studies in geography (4) and geology (6) were produced after 1961. The remaining classifications range in output from one (urban and regional planning) to 13 (drama and theater) and are surely worthy of more intensive research: agriculture and forestry, anthropology, art and architecture, and communications (cinema, press, propaganda, radio and television, music and dance, public health, medicine and nursing, religion and religious history, science, and sports and recreation). The seventies, eighties, and the first years of the nineties witnessed the entry of women on a large scale into doctoral research on Cuba, producing 263 dissertations. Literature was the major interest with over a half in this area alone (154) and history and politics emerging next with a total of 48. These were the areas in which female interest dominated. Their studies in education and psychology deal mostly with Cuban-Americans. Economics, religion, and sciences were under-represented by women.

In a recent study of *Doctoral Research on Puerto Rico and Puerto Ricans*, the author observes that more than half of the 1,650 dissertations accepted by North American, British, and Canadian universities was produced by Puerto Rican scholars from the island. Unfortunately, for this work on Cuban doctoral research, Cuban scholars residing in Cuba who might have completed their doctoral studies in North American graduate schools were denied this opportunity after 1959. As a result, we also were denied the fruits of this possible doctoral research in areas where research has been limited so far as in Cuban anthropology, art, economics, education, music, and science (botany, entomology, marine sciences). For example, in art only one dissertation is listed, the study of the early works of Wilfredo Lam, and in architecture, there is only one dissertation, a study of early nineteenth century residences in central Cuba. On the other hand, the limited number of dissertations produced before 1959 perhaps means the opportunities provided for transplanted Cuban youths enabled them to pursue graduate studies more easily in this environment than if they had remained in Cuba. An examination of the names of the authors of all the dissertations shows that only nine Hispanics produced dissertations prior to 1959. Slightly more than a third of the total number of dissertations accepted in the sixties, seventies, and eighties were produced by Hispanics, almost all of whom we can assume were Cuban Americans by the nature of their topics. Of these, 25 were produced in the sixties, with the very large remainder produced in the seventies and eighties. The conclusion should not be drawn, however, that this constitutes the total amount of doctoral research in which Cuban Americans have been engaged up to the present. Many doctorates have been granted to Cuban Americans whose research projects in the humanities and social sciences have been in areas in which Cuba or Cuban Americans do not figure per se. Hopefully, the time will come when scholars once again will have the opportunity to study first hand the areas that have been neglected far too long.

AGRICULTURE AND FORESTRY

1. Bernstein, Richard Eric. "Land Reform and Resource Allocation in Cuban and Brazilian Agriculture," Brown, 1973.

2. Kanowski, P.J. "Characterization and Interpretation of Variation in Forest Trees: A Reappraisal Based on a Progeny Test of *Pinus Caribaea* Morelet," Oxford, 1986.

3. Meurs, Mieke E. "Participation, Planning and Material Incentives: The Case of Cuban Agriculture in the 1980's," Massachusetts, 1989.

4. Smith, Earl Emmett, Jr. "The Forests of Cuba," Harvard, 1953.

5. Stabler, George Miller. "Bejucal: Social Values and Changes in Agricultural Practices in a Cuban Urban Community," Michigan State, 1958.

See Also Agricultural Economics, Nos. 56-59 and No. 252.

ANTHROPOLOGY

6. Daniel, Yvonne La Verne Payne. "Ethnography of Rumba: Dance and Social Change in Contemporary Cuba," California, Berkeley, 1989.

7. Hahn, Paul Gene, "A Relative Chronology of the Cuban Non-Ceramic Tradition," Yale, 1961.

8. Hulse, Frederick Seymour. "The Comparative Anthropometry of Cubans and Andalusians: A Monograph." Harvard, 1934.

9. Rivero de la Calle, M. "Deformación Craneana en los Aborigínes de Cuba, Estudio Comparativo." Habana, 1949.

See also Sociology and Cultural Anthropology.

ART AND ARCHITECTURE

10. Daniel, Suzanne Garrigues. "The Early Works of Wilfredo Lam, 1941-1945." Maryland, 1983.

11. Garnsey, Clarke Henderson. "Early XIX Century Residences in Central Cuba: The Trinitarian Style." Case Western Reserve, 1962.

See also No. 861.

MASS COMMUNICATIONS

Cinema

12. Hall, Kenneth Estes. "The Function of Cinema in the Works of Guillermo Cabrera Infante and Manuel Puig." Arizona, 1986.

13. López, Ana M. "Towards a 'Third' and 'Imperfect' Cinema: A Theoretical and Historical Study of Filmmaking in Latin America." Iowa, 1986. [Argentina, Brazil and Cuba]

14. Navarro, Lenore Mary. "From Fiction to Film: A Critical Analysis of Graham Greene's *The Fallen Idol* and *Our Man in Havana*, Directed by Carol Reed." Southern California, 1976.

Drama and Theater

15. Arrom, José Juan. "Bosquejo Histórico del Teatro en Cuba (Desde sus Origines hasta 1868)." Yale, 1941.

16. De la Campa, Román Vito. "The Creole Theatre of José Triana: Ritual and Cuban Society." Minnesota, 1975.

17. Edwards, Flora Mancuso. "The Theater of the Black Diaspora: A Comparative Study of Black Drama in Brazil, Cuba and the United States." New York, 1975.

18. Elliott, Norma Jean. "Spanish American Contemporary Political Theatre: 1959-1970." Ohio State, 1980.

19. Franklin, Lillian Cleamons. "The Image of the Black in the Cuban Theater: 1913-1965." Ohio State, 1982.

20. Fuentes, Orliario. "El Teatro de Virgilio Piñera," CUNY, 1985.

21. Goldsmith, Margaret Poynter. "Playwrights of the Cuban Revolution." Cornell, 1975.

22. González, María del Carmen. "La Cultura Popular en el Drama Cubano del Siglo XX." Florida, 1984.

23. Lawrence, Luis S. Chesney. "El Teatro Popular Contemporneo en América Latina, 1955-1985." Southhampton, 1987 [Escambray Theater Group].

24. Melendez, Priscilla. "El Espejo en las Tablas: Teatralidad y Autoconciencia en el Teatro Hispano-Americano Contempornea. "Cornell, 1985 [José Triana].

25. Palls, Terry Lee. "The Theatre in Revolutionary Cuba: 1959-1969." Kansas, 1975.

8 JESSE J. DOSSICK

26. Rodríguez, Teresa Bolet. "Modalidades del Caso y del Proceso Jurídico en el Drama Hispanoamericáno." Iowa, 1986 (Argentina, Costa Rica, Cuba and Mexico).

See also Nos. 606, 610, 672.

The Press

27. Buckman, Robert Thomas. "Comparative Cultural Influences in the Latin American Print Media: A Content Analysis." Texas, 1986.

28. Pierce, Robert Nash. "Public Opinion and Press Opinion in Four Latin American Cities." Minnesota, 1968. [Attitudes toward Castro]

29. Wolfe, Mansell Wayne. "Images of the United States in the Hispanic American Press: A Content Analysis of News and Opinions of This Country Appearing in Daily Newspapers from Nineteen Latin American Republics." Indiana, 1963.

See also Cuba and the American Press, Nos. 353-360, Revistas Nos. 494-498, No. 671 and No. 874.

Propaganda

30. Dickson, Thomas Victor. "Cuba's Attitude Toward the United States as Indicated by Its Use of Propaganda Symbols." Oklahoma State, 1984.

31. Wilkerson, Marcus Manley. "Public Opinion and the Spanish-American War: A Study in War Propaganda." Wisconsin, 1931.

See also No. 341.

Radio and Television

32. Frederick, Howard Handthorne. "Ideology in International Telecommunication: Radio Wars Between Cuba and the United States." American, 1984.

33. Gallimore, Timothy. "Radio Martí: A Case Study of U.S. National Broadcasting Policy and Government Speech in the Marketplace of Ideas," Indiana, 1990.

34. Soruco, Gonzalo Rafael. "Marketing Television Programs in the United States: The Case of the Hispanic Audience." Indiana, 1985.

35. Torres, Alicia Maria. "Presidential Television in the Reagan Era: Network Coverage of Cuba's Role in the Central America Conflict, 1981-1984," Texas, 1989.

36. Werthein, Jorge Ricardo. "A Comparative Analysis of Educational Television in El Salvador and Cuba." Stanford, 1977.

ECONOMICS

General

37. Bernardo, Roberto Medina. "Central Planning in Cuba: Ideology, Structure, and Performance." California, Berkeley, 1967.

38. Geiger, Linwood Townsend. "An Economic Analysis of Expropriation." Temple, 1977.

39. Herrera, A.J. "Cuba: A Prologue to Socialism." Liverpool, 1978.

40. Losman, Donald Lee. "International Economic Systems: The Boycotts of Cuba, Israel, and Rhodesia." Florida, 1969.

41. Ritter, Archibald Robert Milne. "The Economic Development of Revolutionary Cuba: Strategy and Performance." Texas, 1973.

42. Roca, Sergio. "Economic Structure and Ideology in Socialist Cuba." Rutgers, 1975.

See also Nos. 316, 321.

Economic History

43. Batie, Robert Carlyle. "A Comparative Economic History of the Spanish, French, and English on the Caribbean

Islands During the Seventeenth Century." Washington, Seattle, 1972.

44. Denslow, David Albert, Jr. "Sugar Production in North-eastern Brazil and Cuba, 1858-1908." Yale, 1974.

45. Díaz, Manuel Orlando. "The Spanish Average System: An Insurance Scheme and a Loss Prevention Technique Against Piracy Applied in Trade Between Spain and Its American Colonies (Indies) from 1521 to 1660." Pennsylvania, 1960.

46. Ely, Roland Taylor. "From Country House to Cane Field: Moses Taylor and the Cuban Sugar Planter in the Reign of Isabel II, 1833-1868," Harvard, 1959.

47. Fast, J.S. "Monopoly Capital and Empire: The Sugar Trust and American Imperialism, 1883-1909." London, 1976.

48. Fernández, Susan Jane. "Banking, Credit, and Colonial Finance in Cuba, 1878-1895." Florida, 1987.

49. Goizueta Mimó, Félix M. "Effects of Sugar Monoculture upon Colonial Cuba." Pennsylvania, 1971.

50. Hoernel, Robert Bruce. "A Comparison of Sugar and Social Change in Puerto Rico and Oriente, Cuba, 1848-1959." Johns Hopkins, 1977.

51. Hunter, John M. "A Case Study of the Economic Development of an Under-Developed Country __ Cuba, 1899-1935." Harvard, 1951.

52. Pellet, Pedro Fernando. "Socio-Economic Models and the Impacts of a Small Socialist Economy on an Industrialized Society: The Cases of Cuba and the USSR in Historical Perspective." University of Miami, 1986.

53. Surrey, Nancy Maria Miller. "The Commerce of Louisiana During the French Régime, 1699-1763." Columbia, 1916.

54. Wallich, Henry Christopher. "Monetary Problems of an Export Economy: The Cuban Experience, 1914-1942." Harvard, 1944.

55. Westfall, Loy Glenn. "Don Vicente Martínez Ybor, the Man and His Empire: Development of the Clear Havana Industry in Cuba and Florida in the Nineteenth Century." Florida, 1977.

See also Nos. 152, 321, 326, 424, 880.

Agricultural Economics

56. Jones, D.B. "The World Sugar Market, 1950-1965." Oxford, 1969.

57. Sánchez, Nicolás. "The Economics of Sugar Quotas." Southern California, 1972.

58. Smith, Samuel Ivan. "Climatic Control of Distribution and Cultivation of Sugar Cane." McGill, 1964.

59. Vraz, Victor Edgar. "Cuba's Sugar Dilemma in 1931." Northwestern, 1932.

See also Nos. 383-388.

Banking and Finance

60. Leon, Charles F. "The National Bank of Cuba: A Study in Institutional Change." New York, 1964.

Industry

61. Pérez Lopez, Jorge F. "An Index of Cuban Industrial Output, 1930-1958." SUNY, Albany, 1974.

See also No. 66.

Labor

62. Cordova, Efren. "Fidel Castro and the Cuban Labor Movement: 1959-1961." Cornell, 1977.

63. Mesa Lago, Carmelo. "Unemployment in Socialist Countries: Soviet Union, East Europe, China and Cuba." Cornell, 1968.

64. Page, Charles A. "The Development of Organized Labor in Cuba." California, Berkeley, 1952.

65. Pfaller, Alfred. "Labor Demands and the Politics of Economic Development: A Theoretical Framework and

a Comparative Study of Argentina, Bolivia and Cuba."
Pittsburgh, 1973.

66. Stubbs, Jean. "The Cuban Tobacco Industry and Its
Workers, 1860-1958." London, 1975.

See also No. 275, 298, 350.

Tariffs and Trade

67. Glaser, John Stephen. "Organizing International Trade:
The Havana Conference and UNCTAD." Harvard, 1972.

68. Seyed Muhammad, V.A.A. "The General Agreement in
Tariffs and Trade and the Havana Charter." London, 1953.

See also No. 887.

Political Economy

69. O'Connor, James Richard. "The Political Economy of
Pre-Revolutionary Cuba." Columbia, 1965.

See also No. 324. and No. 896.

Economics and Cubans in the United States

70. Carballosa, Evis Louis. "Attitude of the Refugees Toward
Economic Changes in Cuba Since Castro." Texas Christian, 1970.

71. Moncarz, Raúl. "A Study of the Effect of Environmental
Change of Human Capital Among Selected Skilled Cubans," Florida State, 1969.

72. Rodríguez, Leonardo. "An Exploratory Analysis of the
Relationship Between the Application of Organization
Principles and Financial Measures of Success in Cuban
Owned Businesses in Miami, Florida." Florida State, 1975.

73. Santos, Richard. "An Analysis of Earnings Among Persons
of Spanish Origin in the Midwest." Michigan State, 1977.

EDUCATION

General

74. Jackson, Sandra Carter. "Women in Development: A Study of Access to Education and Work in Tanzania and Cuba, 1960-1980." California, Berkeley, 1987.

75. Puroff, Thomas C. "The Cuban National Literary Campaign, 1961," Tennessee, 1972.

76. Templin, Carl Herbert. "A Model of Educational Systems in Revolutionary Societies: China (1949-1974) and Cuba (1959-1981)." Pittsburgh, 1983.

History of Education

77. Abel, James Frederick. "National Ministries of Education." George Washington, 1930.

78. Camper, Natalie K. "Cuba's Post-Revolutionary Work-Study Education: 1959-1975: History, Ideology and Implementation." Boston College, 1979.

79. Fitchen, Edward Douglass. "Alexis Everett Frye and the Organization of Cuban Education: 1899-1901." California, Santa Barbara, 1970.

80. Gumbs, Wycherley Valentine. "Social and Educational Change in a Revolutionary Society: Grenada 1930-1981." Pittsburgh, 1982 [China, Cuba and Grenada].

81. Read, Gerald Howard. "Civic-Military Rural Education in Cuba: Eleven Eventful Years, 1936-1946." Ohio State, 1950.

82. Rodríguez Fraticelli, Carlos. "Education, Politics and Imperialism: The Reorganization of the Cuban Elementary School System During the First American Occupation, 1899-1902." California, San Diego, 1984.

Higher Education

83. Alonso, Miriam G. "La Autonomía Universitaria en América Latina." Catholic, 1969.

84. Follette, Marguerite Ann. "A Study of the Pontifical University in the New World." Catholic, 1967.

See also No. 292.

Education of Cubans in the United States

General

85. Alvarez, Rolando. "Proactive Facilitation with Refugee/Immigrant Students: An Attrition Prevention Study." University of Miami, 1988.

86. Arnes, Jonathan F. "Ideology and Social Studies Textbooks Used in the Education of Hispanic Americans." Wisconsin, 1988 [Florida, Texas and California].

87. Brainard, Clarice H. "A Comparison of the Attitudes Toward Bilingual Education of Cuban, Mexican-American, Puerto Rican and Anglo Parents in Palm Beach County, Florida." Florida State, 1977.

88. Castellanos, Diego Antonio. "The History of Bilingual Education in New Jersey: Its Implications for the Future of Educational Equity for National Origin Students." Fairleigh-Dickenson, 1979.

89. Cruz, Juan Sanjurjo. "Study of Puerto Rican, Mexican, and Cuban Parents' Views on Bilingual/Bicultural Education." Northwestern, 1977 [Chicago].

90. Gomula, Wanda Wallace. "Common Patterns of Non-verbal Behavior Among Selected Cuban and Anglo Children." Indiana, 1973.

91. Hashmi, Aliya. "Post-Migration Investment in Education by Immigrants in the United States." Illinois, Chicago, 1987.

92. Mick, Delores (Lori) Bell. "Assessment Procedures and Enrollment Patterns of Hispanic Students in Special Education and Gifted Programs." Ohio State, 1982.

93. Rosenberg, Emile. "Education of Non-English Speaking Students in America," Boston University, 1974.

94. Serrano, Cheryl Jean. "The Effectiveness of Cross-Level Peer Involvement in the Acquisition of English as a Second Language by Spanish Speaking Migrant Children." Florida State, 1987.

95. Volpe, Arturo. "Public School Superintendents of Spanish Origin or Descent: A Study of Their Background and Selected Conditions in the School Systems They Administer." Northwestern, 1976.

96. Zisman, Paul M. "Education and Economic Success of Urban Spanish-Speaking Immigrants," Catholic, 1973.

See also Nos. 765, 768.

Elementary Education

97. Bass, Bernice Marie. "Oral English Language Assessment of First Grade Children in Bilingual Bicultural Education: Emphasis on Phonology and Syntax." Florida, 1976.

98. Cruz, Julio. "An Exploratory Study of School Climate as Perceived by Teachers in Selected Elementary Schools of an Urban School District Serving Hispanic Students." Peabody College, Vanderbilt, 1986.

99. Herr, Selma Ernestine. "The Effect of Pre-First Grade Training Upon Reading Readiness and Reading Achievement Among Spanish American Children in the First Grade." Texas, 1945.

100. Kinsey, Constance Cooke. "Effects of an Assisted Reading Program on Reading Achievement, Listening Comprehension, and Attitude Toward Reading on Bilingual and Monolingual Primary Children." Washington State, 1985 [Miami].

101. Mack, Mary T. "The Effect of a Curriculum Designed to Improve the Self-Concept and English Oral Language Skills of Spanish-Speaking Migrant Children in the First Grade." Florida, 1981.

102. Morris, Ramona Perkins. "Self-Concept and Ethnic Group Mixture Among Hispanic Students in Elementary Schools." Columbia, 1974 [New York City].

103. Pando, Ana Maria. "Self-Concept, Behavior and Academic Achievement of Anglo-American and Cuban-American Students." Florida, 1988 [4th and 5th grades, Dade County].

104. Richardson, Mabel Wilson, "An Evaluation of Certain Aspects of the Academic Achievement of Elementary Pupils in a Bilingual Program," University of Miami, 1968.

105. Teitel, Raquel S. "Cognitive Functioning, Bilinguality, and Socio-Economic Factors among Spanish-Speaking Children in the District of Columbia," American, 1973.

See also No. 870.

Secondary Education

106. Collins, Brendan M. "A Study of the Relationship of Alienation to the Constructs of Inclusion, Achievement and Affiliation in a Selected Private School." University of Miami, 1980 [Dade County].

107. Fradd, Sandra Homlar. "Language Acquisition of 1980 Cuban Immigrant Junior High School Students."Florida, 1983.

108. Galindo, Hugo Cornelio. "The Effect of Special Language Programs on School Academic Performance of Hispanic High School Students." George Mason, 1989.

109. Hernández, Anthony Cruz-Rivera. "Puerto Rican, Chicano, and Euro-American High School Students' Educational Expectations: A Longitudinal Analysis," California, Los Angeles, 1990.

110. Hynes, Mary Ellen. "An Analysis of Cuban and Non-Cuban Parental Attitudes Toward Public Secondary Education Using Taxonomized Response Options." Kent State, 1974.

111. Lord, Carmen Betancourt. "The Relationship of Maternal Employment and Ethnic Origin to the Sex Role Perception of Cuban-American and Anglo-American Female Adolescents." University of Miami, 1980.

112. Marina, Dorita Roca. "Effects of Culture Conflict of a Structured Intervention Program with Cuban Youth." University of Miami, 1975 [Dade County].

113. Martínez, Juan Carlos. "Student Characteristics and Curricular Patterns in an Urban High School." Boston University, 1984 [Northeast].

114. Meads, Katherine Ann. "The Effects of Two Curricular Approaches on Junior High Students' Attitudes Towards Hispanics." Florida State, 1988.

115. Rossell, Ana E. "Acculturation of Hispanic Adolescent Students." Hofstra, 1985 [New York City].

116. Shu, Gang Jian. "The Determinants of Dropping Out of High Schools for Cuban Americans, Mexican Americans and Puerto Ricans," Wisconsin, 1988.

Higher Education

117. Arnov, Venice Beaulieu. "Analysis of the Effects of Language on Impression Formation: Evaluation Reactions of Miami-Dade Community College Students to the Voices of Cuban-Americans Speaking in English and in Spanish." Florida Atlantic, 1978.

118. Borunda, Mario Rene. "Emerging Hispanic Colleges and Universities," Harvard, 1990. [one in Miami]

119. Butterwick, John Teasdale. "A Dimensional Comparison of the Political Cultures of Cuban and American Community College Students in the Miami Area." University of Miami, 1973.

120. Calderón, Jaime Abdom. "Cuban-Americans' Perceptions of College-going and the Intention to Persist at the University." Houston, 1988 [Southeastern U.S.].

121. Coppolechia, Yillian Castro. "Bilingual and Monolingual Instruction: A Comparison of Performance Outcomes Among College Level Spanish-Speaking Students." University of Miami, 1984 [Cubans in Miami].

122. Davis, J. Michael. "The Relationship of Selection Factors in the Cuban Teacher Retraining Program to the Effective Classroom Performance of Cuban Teachers." University of Miami, 1969.

123. Davis, John Mathew. "Student Affairs at the University of Florida as Perceived by Black, Cuban and White Students of Both Sexes." Florida, 1975.

124. Elie, Gerri Moore. "Environmental Perceptions, Stress Levels, and Demographic Conditions Affecting Black, Hispanic, and White Graduate Students," Florida, 1989.

125. Isern, Margarita. "An Investigation of Bias in Tests of Writing Ability for Bilingual Hispanic College Students," University of Miami, 1986.

126. Khouzam, Nevine Nagui. "The Adjustment Process of Hispanic Students at the University of Florida, 1985-1986," Florida, 1986.

127. Maspons, Maria Mercedes. "Pre-training Hispanic Students on Test-Taking Strategies and Its Effects on the Reliability and Predictive Validity of a Mathematics Predictor Test," University of Miami, 1983.

128. Migdail, Sherry Resnick. "An Analysis of Current Select Teacher Training Programs in Bilingual/Bicultural Education and the Development of New Teacher-Training Designs," American, 1976.

129. Richardson, Raysa Carregado. "The Relationship of Ethnic Group Membership, Age, Sex, Achievement and Locus-of-Control to the Self-Report of a Group of Cuban Students in the University of Florida," Florida, 1976.

130. Roca, Ana. "Pedagogical and Sociolinguistic Perspectives on the Teaching of Spanish to Hispanic Bilingual College

Students in South Florida," University of Miami, 1986. [Miami]

131. Santiago, Emelina. "Perceived Factors that Influence Enrollment Decisions of Hispanic Students at the Florida State University," Florida State, 1990.

132. Sevick, Charles Vincent. "A History and Evaluation of the Cuban Teacher Retraining Program of the University of Miami, 1963-1973," University of Miami, 1974.

133. Smith, Juel Hickman Shannon. "Student Use of Support Services, Involvement and Satisfaction with the University Environment: A Comparative Study of Black, Caucasian and Hispanic Undergraduate Students," South Florida, 1987.

134. Spiro, Loida Velzquez. "Accessibility of Higher Education for Hispanic Students," Temple, 1985.

135. Spoto, Elizabeth Josephine. "A Comparative Study of Value Systems Among Black, Hispanic, and White Community College Students," Florida, 1978.

136. Younkin, William F. "Speededness as a Source of Test Bias for Non-Native English Speakers on the College Level Academic Skills Test," University of Miami, 1986.

See also No. 891

GEOGRAPHY

137. Chamberlin, Thomas W. "Phases of the Urban and Industrial Geography of Havana, Cuba." Clark, 1946.

138. Hayford, Alison Margaret. "The Territory of Struggle: A Political Geography of Revolution." Michigan, 1981.

139. Winsberg, Morton Daniel. "The Isle of Pines, Cuba: A Geographic Interpretation." Florida, 1958.

140. Wright, A. Joseph. "A Climatic Survey of Cuba," Clark, 1951.

See also No. 423.

GEOLOGY

141. Guild, Philip White. "Petrology and Structure of the Moa Chromite District, Oriente Province, Cuba," Johns Hopkins, 1947.

142. Hewitt, Philip Cooper, "Larger Foraminifera of Certain Eocene and Oligocene Formations of Cuba," Cornell, 1958.

143. Hill, Patrick Arthur. "The Geology of Mineralization and Leached Outcrops of the Minas Carlota Region, Las Villas, Cuba," Columbia, 1958.

144. Kozary, Myron Theodore. "Conglomerates Associated with the Cubitas Plateau, Cuba," Columbia, 1954.

145. Purdom, William Berlin. "Geology of the Minera Occidental Bosch, S.A. and the Coto Francisco, Pinar del Río, Cuba," Arizona, 1961.

146. Roesler, Max. "Geology of the Iron-Ore Deposits of the Firmeza District, Oriente Province, Cuba," Yale, 1916.

HISTORY

-1800

147. Aimes, Hubert Hillary Suffern. "A History of Slavery in Cuba, 1511 to 1868," Yale, 1905.

148. Brown, Genevieve. "Illicit Slave Trade to Cuba and Other Islands of the Caribbean," Ohio State, 1945.

149. Corbitt, Duvon Clough. "The Colonial Government of Cuba," North Carolina, 1939.

150. Cummins, Light Townsend. "Spanish Agents in North America during the Revolution, 1775-1779," Tulane, 1977.

151. Cunningham, Charles Henry. "The Audiencia in Spanish Colonies," California, Berkeley, 1915.

152. De La Pedraja Toman, René Andrés, "Politics and the Economy in the Hispanic Antilles, 1789-1820," Chicago, 1977.

153. Gunst, Laurie Barbara. "Bartolomé de las Casas and the Question of Slavery in the Early Spanish Indies," Harvard, 1982.

154. Haring, Clarence Henry. "Trade and Navigation Between Spain and the Indies in the Time of the Hapsburgs," Harvard, 1916.

155. Inglis, Gordon Douglas. "Historical Demography of Colonial Cuba, 1492-1780," Texas Christian, 1979.

156. Jensen, Larry Russell. "The Mania to Write and Read: Culture and Repression in Colonial Cuba, 1790-1840," Stanford, 1981.

157. Lampros, Peter James. "Merchant-Planter Cooperation and Conflict: the Havana Consulado, 1794-1832," Tulane, 1980.

158. McNeil, John Robert. "Theory and Practice in the Bourbon Empires of the Atlantic: The Roles of Louisbourg and Havana, 1713-1763," Duke, 1981.

159. Morales, José. "The Hispanic Diaspora, 1791-1850: Puerto Rico, Cuba, Louisiana, and Other Host Societies," Connecticut, 1986.

160. Salvucci, Linda Kerrigan. "Development and Decline: The Port of Philadelphia and Spanish Imperial Markets, 1783-1823," Princeton, 1985.

See also Nos. 53, 163.

1801-1867

161. Bradford, Richard Headlee. "The Virginius Affair: A Study in Crisis Diplomacy," Indiana, 1973.

162. Caldwell, Robert Granville. "The López Expeditions to Cuba 1848-1851," Princeton, 1912.

163. Del Ducca, Gemma Marie. "A Political Portrait: Félix Varela y Morales, 1788-1853," New Mexico, 1966.

164. Diket, Albert L. "John Slidell and the Community He Represented in the Senate, 1853-1861," Lousiana State, 1958.

165. Ettinger, Amos A. "The Mission to Spain of Pierre Soulé, 1853-55: A Study in the Cuban Diplomacy of the United States with Special Reference to Contemporary Opinion," Oxford, 1930.

166. Griffin, Charles Carroll. "The United States and the Disruption of the Spanish Empire, 1810-1822: A Study of the Relations of the United States with Spain and with the Rebel Spanish Colonies," Columbia, 1937.

167. Hall, Gwendolyn Midlo. "Social Control in Slave Plantation Societies: A Comparison of St. Dominique and Cuba," Michigan, 1970.

168. Howard, Philip Anthony. "Culture, Nationalism, and Liberation: The Afro-Cuban Mutual Aid Societies in the Nineteenth Century," Indiana, 1988.

169. Kiple, Kenneth Franklin. "The Cuban Slave Trade, 1820-1862: The Demographic Implications for Comparative Studies," Florida, 1970.

170. Knight, Franklin Willis. "Cuban Slave Society on the Eve of Abolition, 1830-1880," Wisconsin, 1969.

171. Kyle, Joseph B. "Spain and Its Colonies, 1814-1820," Duke, 1952.

172. Langnas, A.J. "The Relations Between Great Britain and the Spanish Colonies, 1808-1812," London, 1938.

173. Leard, Robert B. "Bonds of Destiny: The United States and Cuba, 1848-1861," California, Berkeley, 1954.

174. MacMaster, Richard Kerwin. "The United States, Great Britain and the Suppression of the Cuban Slave Trade, 1830-1860," Georgetown, 1968.

175. Martínez-Fernández, Luis. "The Hispanic Caribbean Between Empires, 1840-1868", Duke, 1990.

176. Meagher, Arnold Joseph. "The Introduction of Chinese Laborers to Latin America: The Coolie Trade, 1847-1874," California, Davis, 1975.

177. Murray, David Robert. "Britain, Spain and the Slave Trade to Cuba, 1807-1845," Cambridge, 1968.

178. Paquette, Robert Louis. "The Conspiracy of La Escalera: Colonial Society and Politics in Cuba in the Age of Revolution," Rochester, 1982".

179. Philbrick, Francis Samuel. "The Relations of the United States and Cuba to 1830," Harvard, 1902.

180. Potter, Kenneth. "The Hispanic American Policy of John Quincy Adams, 1817-1825," California, Berkeley, 1934.

181. Poyo, Gerald Eugene. "Cuban Emigré Communities in the United States and the Independence of Their Homeland, 1852-1895," Florida, 1983.

182. Rauch, Basil. "American Interest in Cuba: 1848-1855," Columbia, 1946.

183. Roberts, Harmon Martin, Jr. "The Revival of Spain and the Development of Cuba, 1823-1830," University of Miami, 1977.

184. Smith, Arthur Francis. "Spain and the Problem of Slavery in Cuba, 1817-1873," Chicago, 1958.

185. Solnick, Bruce B. "American Opinion Concerning the Spanish-American Wars of Independence, 1808-1824," New York, 1961.

24 JESSE J. DOSSICK

186. Whalen, Wickie Burton. "José Antonio Saco, Cuban Reformer, 1797-1879," University of Miami, 1970.

See also Nos. 147, 152, 157, 159, 790, 872.

1868-1894

187. Baker, Thomas Hart, Jr. "Imperial Finale: Crises, De-Colonization, and War in Spain, 1890-1898," Princeton, 1977.

188. Belcher, Jack Benjamin. "Economic Initiatives of the United States Congress on American Foreign Policy, 1886-1896: A Quantitative Analysis," Georgetown, 1976.

189. Delgado, Octavio Avelino. "The Spanish Army in Cuba, 1868-1898: An Institutional Study," Columbia, 1980.

190. Dozer, Donald M. "Anti-Imperialism in the United States, 1865-1895," Harvard, 1936.

191. Ellmore, Winant Stubbs. "Diplomatic Background of the Spanish American War: The Cuban Question," Georgetown, 1956.

192. Gray, Richard Butler. "José Martí: His Life, Ideas, Apotheosis and Significance as a Symbol in Cuban Politics and Selected Social Organizations," Wisconsin, 1957.

193. Jacobs, C.C. "The Diplomatic History of the Cuban Ten Years' War, 1868-1873," Birmingham, 1975.

194. Kirk, John Michael. "The Socio-Political Thought of José Martí: His Plans for the Liberated *Patria*," British Columbia, 1977.

195. Lambert, F.J.D. "The Cuban Question in Spanish Restoration Politics, 1878-1898," Oxford, 1969.

196. Mestas, Juan Eugenio. "José Martí: Su Concepto de la Clase Obrera." SUNY, Stony Brook, 1985.

197. Nichols, Lawrence R. "The Bronze Titan: The Mulatto Hero of the Cuban Independence, Antonio Maceo," Duke, 1954.

198. Oria, Tomás. "Martí, el Moralista del Krausismo," Massachusetts, 1980.

199. Parker, Ralph Halstead. "Imperialism and Liberation of Cuba, 1868-1898," Texas, 1935.

200. Powers, Marshall Kent. "Chinese Coolie: Migration to Cuba," Florida, 1953.

201. Rigby, Barry Ross. "American Expansion in the Pacific and Caribbean Islands, 1865-1877," Duke, 1978.

202. Scott, Rebecca Jarvis. "Slave Emancipation and the Transition to Free Labor in Cuba, 1868-1895," Princeton, 1982.

203. True, Marshall MacDonald. "Revolutionaries in Exile: The Cuban Revolutionary Party, 1891-1898," Virginia, 1965.

See also Nos. 160, 168, 170, 176, 218, 634, 872.

1895-1903

204. Barnes, Arthur M. "American Intervention in Cuba and Annexation of the Philippines, An Analysis of the Public Discussion," Cornell, 1948.

205. Cosmas, Graham Athan. "An Army for Empire: The United States Army in the Spanish-American War, 1898-1899," Wisconsin, 1969.

206. Crouch, Thomas William. "The Making of a Soldier: The Career of Frederick Funston, 1865-1902," Texas, 1969.

207. Duncan, George William. "The Diplomatic Career of William Rufus Day, 1897-1898," Case Western Reserve, 1976.

208. Gianakos, Perry Edgar. "'The Yanko-Spanko War': Our War With Spain in American Fiction," New York, 1961.

209. Halkiotis, Stephen Herman. "Neutrality and Enforcement: The U.S.A. and Cuban Filibustering, 1895-1898," North Carolina, 1976.

210. Harper, James William. "Hugh Lenox Scott: Soldier, Diplomat, 1876-1917," Virginia, 1968.

211. Healy, David Frank. "The Formation of America's Cuban Policy, 1898-1902," Wisconsin, 1961.

212. Hitchman, James Harold. "Leonard Wood and the Cuban Question, 1898-1902," California, Berkeley, 1975.

213. Lashley, Warren L. "The Debate Over Imperialism in the United States, 1898-1900," Northwestern, 1966.

214. Maza, Miguel Manuel P. "Between Ideology and Compassion: The Cuban Insurrection of 1895-98, Through the Private Correspondence of Cuba's Two Prelates with the Holy See," Georgetown, 1987.

215. Meyer, Leo J. "Relations Between the United States and Cuba From 1895 to 1917," Clark, 1928.

216. Newton, Irene E. "The Treaty of Paris of 1898," California, Berkeley, 1927

217. Pons, Alexandre. "La Question de Cuba au point de vue du droit international," Montpelier, 1906.

218. Preece, Carol Ann Aiken. "Insurgent Guests: The Cuban Revolutionary Party and Its Activities in the United States, 1892-1898," Georgetown, 1976.

219. Reuter, Bertha Ann. "Anglo-American Relations During the Spanish-American War," Iowa, 1923.

220. Reynolds, Bradley Michael. "Guantanamo Bay, Cuba: The History of an American Naval Base and Its Relationship to the Formation of United States Foreign Policy and Military Strategy Toward the Caribbean, 1895-1910," Southern California, 1982.

221. Ruff, Thomas Peter. "Indiana's Reaction to the Cuban Crisis, 1895-1898," Ball State, 1968.

222. Schellings, William John. "The Role of Florida in the Spanish-American War, 1898," Florida, 1958.

223. Sfeir-Younis, Luis Felipe. "State Formation in the Periphery: The United States Military Occupation of Cuba and Puerto Rico, 1898-1902," Michigan, 1989.

224. Tejera, Felix C. "An American Dilemma: The Cuban Question, 1895-1897," Florida State, 1975.

225. Villanueva, Honesto Abad. "The Diplomacy of the Spanish-American War," California, Los Angeles, 1941.

226. Weible, Friedrich Viktor. "The Anatomy of United States Imperialism: Cultural Perspectives on American Interventionism in the Western Hemisphere, 1895-1907," Minnesota, 1989

227. Weigle, Richard D. "The Sugar Interests and American Diplomacy in Hawaii and Cuba, 1893-1903," Yale, 1939.

228. Wexler, Alice Ruth. "Historians, Society, and the Spanish-Cuban-American War of 1898," Indiana, 1972.

229. Whitcomb, A. "La situation international de Cuba," Paris, 1905.

230. Wisan, Joseph Ezra. "The Cuban Crisis as Reflected in the New York Press, 1895-1898," Columbia, 1934.

231. Zais, Barrie Emert. "The Struggle For a 20th Century Army: Investigation and Reform of the United States Army after the Spanish-American War, 1898-1903," Duke, 1981.

See also Nos. 187, 203, 233, 245, 336, 794.

1904-1933

232. Aguilar, Luis Enrique. "Cuba, 1933: The Frustrated Revolution," American, 1968.

233. Coski, John Matthew. "The Triple Mandate: The Concept of Trusteeship and American Imperialism, 1898-1934," College of William and Mary, 1987.

234. De Froscia, Patrick David. "The Diplomacy of Elihu Root, 1905-1909," Temple, 1976.

235. Fermoselle López, Rafael. "Black Politics in Cuba: The Race War of 1912," American, 1972.

236. Gómez Camejo, Mario. "Remarque sur la disparation de la fievre jaune Cuba au commencement du XXe siècle," Paris, 1934.

237. Lockmiller, David A. "The Second United States Intervention in Cuba, 1906-1909," North Carolina, 1935.

238. Millett, Allan Reed. "The Politics of Intervention: The Military Occupation of Cuba, 1906-1909," Ohio State, 1966.

239. Mondejar, John Patrick. "Neo-Colonialism as an Economic System: Cuba, 1898-1934," Indiana, 1976.

240. Orum, Thomas Tondee. "The Politics of Color: The Racial Dimension of Cuban Politics During the Early Republican Years 1900-1912," New York, 1975.

241. Pérez, Louis A., Jr. "The Rise and Fall of Army Preeminence in Cuba, 1898-1958," New Mexico, 1971.

242. Rosell, Raúl Gonzalo. "El Ensayo en la Generacíon de 1924 en Cuba," Nebraska, 1973.

243. Rowe, Joseph Milton, Jr. "William Howard Taft: Diplomatic Troubleshooter," Texas A and M, 1977 [1906].

244. Schwartz, Rosalie. "The Displaced and the Disappointed Cultural Nationalists and Black Activists in Cuba in the 1920s," California, San Diego, 1977.

245. Stoner, Kathryn Lynn. "From the House to the Streets: Women's Movement for Legal Change in Cuba, 1898-1958," Indiana, 1983.
See also No. 215.

1934-1958

246. Aaron, Harold Robert. "The Seizure of Political Power in Cuba, 1956-1959," Georgetown, 1964.

247. Badillo, David A. "From South of the Border: Latino Experiences in Urban America," CUNY, 1988 [Chicanos, Cubans and Puerto Ricans, Post World War II].

248. Baloyra, Enrique Antonio. "Political Leadership in the Cuban Republic, 1944-1958," Florida, 1971.

249. Erisman, H. Michael. "Revolution and Revolutionary Elites in Latin America," Pennsylvania State, 1972.

250. Gellman, Irwin Frederick. "Good Neighbor Diplomacy and the Rise of Batista, 1933-1945," Indiana, 1970.

251. Hargrove, Claude. "Fulgencio Batista: Politics of the Electoral Process in Cuba, 1933-1944," Harvard, 1979.

252. Martínez Piedra, Alberto. "Land Reform in Cuba (1933-1958)," Georgetown, 1962.

253. Rys, John Frank. "Tensions and Conflicts in Cuba, Haiti, and the Dominican Republic Between 1945 and 1959," American, 1966.

254. Sadler, Louis Ray. "The Rocambole Conspiracy: The Abortive 1947 Cuban Invasion," South Carolina, 1971.

255. Valdes, Nelson Peter. "The Cuban Rebellion: Internal Organization and Strategy, 1952-1959," New Mexico, 1978.

See also Nos. 245, 306, 354, 814.

1959 -

256. Chaffee, Wilber Albert, Jr. "A Theoretical Look at Revolutions with Case Studies from Latin America," Texas, 1975.

257. Crain, David Allan. "The Course of Cuban Heresy: The Rise and Decline of Castroism's Challenge to the Soviet Line in the Latin American Marxist Revolutionary Movement, 1963-1970," Indiana, 1972.

258. Cruz-Taura, Graciella. "The Impact of the Castro Revolution on Cuban Historiography," University of Miami, 1978.

259. Frederick, D.C. "The Failure of Compliance Strategies: A Comparative Approach to the Iranian, Nicaraguan and Cuban Revolutions," Oxford, 1986.

260. Masud Piloto, Félix Roberto. "The Political Dynamics of the Cuban Migration to the United States, 1959-1980," Florida State, 1985.

261. Padula, Alfred L., Jr. "The Fall of the Bourgeoisie: Cuba, 1959-1961," New Mexico, 1974.

262. Roe, Teddy W. "A Review of Factors Leading to Fidel Castro's Retreat on Armed Struggle, 1967 and 1968," California, San Diego, 1977.

263. Ryan, Jeffrey John. "The Dynamics of Latin American Insurgencies: 1956-1986," Rice, 1989.

264. Weiss, Judith Anne. "*Casa de las Américas*: An Intellectual Review in the Cuban Revolution," Yale, 1973.

POLITICS, THE MILITARY, DIPLOMACY AND FOREIGN RELATIONS

General

265. Assetto, Valerie J. "Communist States in the IMF and IBRD: Conflict and Cooperation," Rice, 1984.

266. Azicri, Max. "A Study of the Structure of Exercizing Power in Cuba: Mobilization and Governing Strategies (1959-1968)," Southern California, 1975.

267. Bwy, Douglas Prieur. "Political Instability in Latin America: A Comparative Study," Northwestern, 1968.

268. Cabrera, Lillian Eleanor. "Character Models of the Cuban Revolutionary Regime," Georgetown, 1981.

269. Chen, Hsiao-Hung Nancy. "The Elusiveness of Administrative Reform Strategies for National Development: A Comparative View," Pittsburgh, 1977.

270. Conklin, John Gordon. "The Latin American Chief Executive," Arizona, 1976.

271. Diamond, Norman William. "The Development of Socialist Consciousness in Cuba," Harvard, 1970.

272. Einaudi, Luigi Roberto. "Marxism in Latin America: From Aprismo to Fidelismo," Harvard, 1967.

273. Evans, Bette Novit. "The Moral Versus Material Incentives Controversy in Cuba: Where Ideology and Public Policy Meet," Pittsburgh, 1973.

274. Falk, Pamela S. "Cuba's Foreign and Domestic Policies, 1968-78: The Effect of International Commitments on Internal Development," New York, 1980.

275. Fuller, Linda Olsen. "The Politics of Workers' Control in Cuba: 1959-1983: The Work Center and the National Arena," California, Berkeley, 1985.

276. Gilbert, Jorge de Jésus. "Cuba: From Primitive Accumulation of Capital to Socialism" Toronto, 1980.

277. Harbert, Joseph R. "The Domestic and International Politics of Internal Conflict: A Comparative Analysis," CUNY, 1984.

278. Harris, Kathy B. "High Physical Life Quality in Poor Countries: The Cases of Cuba and Jamaica," Georgia, 1986.

279. Iglesias, Alex. "Active Resistance as a Major Method of Coping in a Communist Political Prison," Florida, 1984.

280. Jones, Roger Eugene, "The Symbolic Uses of Politics: Examples from Cuba, 1952-1971," University of Miami, 1972.

281. Lanning, Eldon Wayne. "The Bolivian Revolution of 1952 and the Cuban Revolution of 1959: Case Studies of a Theory of Revolution," Virginia, 1965.

282. Leahy, Margaret Ellen. "Equality and Inequality in Capitalist and Socialist Societies: Comparative Studies of Women and National Development in the US, Mexico, the USSR, and Cuba," Southern California, 1981.

283. Leogrande, William Mark. "The Political Institutionalization of Mass-Elite Linkages in Revolutionary Cuba," Syracuse, 1976.

284. Lutjens, Sheryl Lea. "The State, Bureaucracy, and Politics: Administrative Reform in Cuba," California, Berkeley, 1987.

285. Moses, Carl Calvin. "Judicial Control of the Constitutionality of Legislation in Cuba," North Carolina, 1958.

286. Pérez Stable, Marifeli, "Politics and Conciencia in Revolutionary Cuba, 1959-1984," SUNY, Story Brook, 1985.

287. Rabkin, Rhoda Pearl. "Cuban Socialism: A Case Study of Marxist Theory in Practice," Harvard, 1983.

288. Rafat, Amir. "Expropriation of the Private Property of Aliens in Recent International Law: Iran, Egypt, Indonesia, and Cuba," Minnesota, 1965.

289. Ramm, Hartmut. "The Political Philosophy of Regis Debray: Between Lenin and Guevara," Florida State, 1974.

290. Rose, Gregory Frank. "Politics, Games and Culture: A Game-Theoretic Analysis of Political Mobilization by Revolutionary Elites in Iran, Kampuchea, and Cuba," Texas, 1987.

291. Russell, Charles Alvin. "Cuban Theories of Revolutionary War Examined in a Comparative Context," American, 1972.

292. Suchlicki, Jaime. "University of Havana Students and Politics, 1920-1966," Texas Christian, 1967.

293. Tai, Chong Soo. "The Effects of Revolution: A Quasi-Experimental Analysis of Six Revolutions," Northwestern, 1974.

294. Tortolani, Paul J. "Cuba 1959-1970: The Evolution of an Administrative System in a Revolutionary Context," New York, 1979.

295. Tretiak, Daniel. "Perspectives of Cuba's Relations with the Communist System: The Politics of a Communist Independent, 1959-1969," Stanford, 1974.

296. Williams, Richard Clayton. "Social Causes of Violent Revolution in Eighty-Six Nations Since World War II," Colorado, 1978.

297. Ya Deau, A.B. "Terrorism and Guerrilla Warfare: An Essay on People's War and Revolution," Aberdeen, 1986.

298. Zeitlin, Maurice. "Working Class Politics in Cuba: A Study in Political Sociology," California, Berkeley, 1964.

See also Nos. 248, 256, 815, 888.

Fidel Castro

299. Biandudi, Joncker K. Ibn. "A Review of Selected Materials on the Development Strategies of Zhou Enlai, Fidel Castro and Gamal Abdel Nasser," Ohio State, 1984.

300. Brotherson, Festus, Jr. "Understanding Effective Political Leadership in the Third World __ An Alternative approach; the Cases of Fidel Castro and Indira Gandhi," California, Los Angeles, 1985.

301. Edelstein, Joel Calvin. "The Evolution of Goals and Priorities in the Thought of Fidel Castro Ruz," California, Riverside, 1975.

302. Gallagher, Mary Brigid. "The Public Address of Fidel Castro Ruz: Charismatic Leader of a Modern Revolution," Pittsburgh, 1970.

303. Lumsden, Charles Ian. "Consciousness and Conviction: The Political Beliefs of Fidel Castro," Toronto, 1970.

304. Truby, John Orrien. "Levels of Adaptiveness, Trends in Fidel Castro's Calculations Concerning the Promotion of Revolution in Latin America from 1963 through 1972," South Carolina, 1974.

See also Nos. 62, 272, 877, 894.

The Military

305. Hernández, José M. "The Role of the Military in the Making of the Cuban Republic," Georgetown, 1976.

306. Judson, Charles Frederick. "The Development of Revolutionary Myths in the Political Education of the Cuban Rebel Army 1953-1963," Alberta, 1982.

307. Reppert, John Clayton. "The Political Officer in Communist Military Units: Roles and Relationships." George Washington, 1982.

308. Scheina, Robert Lewis. "Indigenous Latin American Sea Power, 1890-1974," Catholic, 1976.

See also Nos. 81, 318.

Cuba and Human Rights

309. Leblanc, Lawrence Joseph. "The OAS and the Promotion and Protection of Human Rights," Iowa, 1973.

310. Schreiber, Anna Panayotou. "The Inter-American Commission on Human Rights," Columbia, 1969.

See also No. 351.

DIPLOMACY AND FOREIGN RELATIONS

The United States and Cuba (See History also)
General

311. Berry, Lee Roy, Jr. "The United States Congress and Cuba: Four Case Studies of Congressional Influence in American Foreign Policy," Notre Dame, 1976.

312. Boynton, Maryanna Craig. "Effects of Embargo and Boycott: The Cuban Case." California, Riverside, 1972.

313. Brown, Douglas Allen. "Three Perspectives on US Foreign Aid: Explaining the Alliance for Progress," Oregon, 1974 [to offset Castroism].

314. Hopf, Carroll Henry. "What An American Should Know About Cuba," Colorado State, 1962.

315. Keagle, James Martin. "Toward an Understanding of US/Latin American Policy," Princeton, 1982.

316. Ruffin, Patricia. "Dependency, Development and Under-Development: A Case Study of the Economic and Political Relations Between the United States, the Soviet Union and Cuba," New School for Social Research, 1986.

317. Shelar, Victoria Dawn. "A Study of Loneliness and Leisure Among Unaccompanied Enlisted Military Personnel Stationed in Guantanamo Bay, Cuba," Maryland, 1988.

318. Smetherman, Bobbie Braly. "United States Military Assistance to Cuba: An American Viewpoint," Claremont, 1967.

319. Wilson, Larman Curtis. "The Principle of Non-Intervention in Recent Interamerican Relations: The Challenge of Anti-Democratic Regimes," Maryland, 1964.

320. Yinger, Jon A. "Cuba: American and Soviet Core Interests in Conflict," Claremont, 1966.

See also No. 32.

1895-1958

General

321. Leroy, Jean Landri. "From Capitalism to Socialism: The Character and the Extent of Cuba's Economic and Political Dependency on the United States and on the Soviet Union, 1900-1980," Pennsylvania, 1985.

322. Maris, Gary Leroy. "Some Aspects of International Law in United States-Cuban Relations: 1898-1964," Duke, 1965.

323. Morley, Morris Hyman. "Toward a Theory of Imperial Politics: United States Policy and the Process of State Formation, Disintegration and Consolidation in Cuba, 1898-1978," SUNY, Binghamton, 1980.

See also No. 889.

1895-1958

324. Benjamin, Jules Robert. "The United States and the Cuban Revolution of 1933: The Role of United States Hegemony in the Cuban Political Economy, 1880-1934, " Pennsylvania, 1974.

325. Diez, William Edwin. "Opposition in the United States to American Diplomacy in the Caribbean, 1898-1932," Chicago, 1946.

326. Figueroa, Javier. "Creating Paradise: The Cuban-American Struggle for Control of Cuba's Economic Development, 1944-1952," Connecticut, 1988.

327. Fitzgibbon, Russell Humke. "Cuba and the United States, 1900-1935," Wisconsin, 1933.

328. Gaylor, Sylvia Katz. "The Abrogation of the Platt Amendment: A Case Study in United States — Cuban Relations, with Special Emphasis on Public Opinion," New York, 1971.

329. Gibean, Victor H., Jr. "Relations of Cuba with the United States, 1916-1921," North Carolina, 1954.

330. Jackman, Francis V. "America's Cuban Policy During the Period of the Machado Regime," Catholic, 1965.

331. Kesler, John C. "Spruille Braden and Good Neighbor: The Latin American Policy of the United States, 1930-1947," Kent State, 1985.

332. Krogh, Peter Frederic. "Sumner Welles and United States Relations with Cuba: 1933," Tufts, Fletcher School of Law and Diplomacy," 1966.

333. Millington, Thomas Muzzy. "The Latin American Diplomacy of Sumner Welles," Johns Hopkins, 1967.

334. Schwartz, Robert Norman. "Diplomatic Relations with Latin America 1945-1960: The Unsettling Dichotomies of Security and Development," Houston, 1985.

335. Smith, Robert Freeman. "American Business Interests and Cuban-American Relations, 1919-1933," Wisconsin, 1959.

336. Vahle, Cornelius Wendell, Jr. "Congress, the President and Overseas Expansion, 1897-1901," George Washington, 1967.

337. Zoumaras, Thomas. " The Path to Panamericanism: Eisenhower's Foreign Economic Policy Toward Latin America," Connecticut, 1987.

See also Nos. 31, 233, 316, 320, 425.

1959 -

338. Bailey, Jennifer Leigh. "Dependent Revolution: The United States and Radical Change in Bolivia and Cuba," Denver, 1990.

339. Bender, Lynn Darrell. "US-Cuban Relations, 1959-1972: An Examination of the Determinants, Implications, and Consequences of American Policy Toward the Revolutionary Regime," George Washington, 1972.

340. Bonachea, Rolando E. "United States Policy Toward Cuba: 1959-1961," Georgetown, 1976.

341. Brown, Richard Mayhew. "United States Propaganda Performance in Crisis, 1960-1965," North Carolina, 1970.

342. Herr, Donald Furse. "Presidential Influence and Bureaucratic Politics: Nixon's Policy Toward Cuba," Yale, 1978.

343. Hidalgo, Olivia Marsha Hardeman. "Carter, Reagan, and the Cubans: The Impact of Changing Fiscal Policy on Mariel Entrants in Chicago, Illinois," Purdue, 1986.

344. Jervis, David T. "The United States Confronts Change in Latin America," Temple, 1985 [1958-1961].

345. Minter, William Maynard. "The Council of Foreign Relations: A Case Study of the Societal Bases of Foreign Policy Formation," Wisconsin, 1973.

346. Moss, Richard Holland. "The Limits of Policy: An Investigation of the Spiral Model, the Deterrence Model, and Miscalculations in US-Third World Relations," Princeton, 1987.

347. Rivera, Mario Antonio. "An Evaluative Analysis of the Carter Administration's Policy Toward the Mariel Influx of 1980," Notre Dame, 1982.

348. Robbins, Carla Anne. "The Cuban Threat," California, Berkeley, 1982.

349. Tierney, Kevin Beirne. "American-Cuban Relations: 1957-1963," Syracuse, 1979.

350. Torrence, Donald Ray. "American Imperialism and Latin American Labor, 1959-1970: A Study of the Role of the Organizacíon Regional Interamericana de Trabajadores in the Latin American Policy of the United States," Northern Illinois, 1975.

351. Vavrina Vernon, Joseph, Jr. "Human Rights and American Foreign Policy: Violations of the Integrity of the Person, Selected Cases, 1969-1980," Georgetown, 1984.

352. Wright, George Vandergriff. "A Case Study of US Foreign Policy: The Carter Administration and Angola," Leeds, 1987.

See also Nos. 30, 32, 425, 430, 432, 433, 895.

The American Press and Cuba

353. Auxier, George Washington. "The Cuban Question as Reflected in the Editorial Columns of Middle Western Newspapers 1895-1898," Ohio State, 1938.

354. Cooke, Gerald Edward. "News Media Perception and Projection of the Castro Rebellion, 1957-1958: Some Image Theme Affects in the Foreign Policy System," Maryland, 1969.

355. Cozean, Jon Dennis. "The US Elite Press and Foreign Policy: The Case of Cuba," American, 1979.

356. Kern, Montague. "The Presidency and the Press: John F. Kennedy's Foreign Policy Crisis and the Politics of Newspaper Coverage," Johns Hopkins, 1980.

357. Kreisman, Leonard Theodore. "Published Opinion in American Periodicals and Senatorial Opinion," New York, 1955.

358. McNulty, Edward M. "The Cuban Crisis as Reflected in the New Jersey Press, 1895-1898," Rutgers, 1970.

359. Ortiz, Albert Arthur. "Daniel Jarvis: A Cold War Correspondent in Latin America," Washington State, 1988.

360. Welter, Mark Matthew. "Minnesota Newspapers and the Cuban Crisis, 1895-1898: Minnesota as a Test Case for the 'Yellow Journalism' Theory," Minnesota, 1970.

The Bay of Pigs

361. Barilleaux, Ryan John. "The Presidential Ordeal: Evaluating Performance in Foreign Affairs," Texas, 1983.

362. Stuart, Douglas Thomas. "The Relative Potency of Leader Beliefs as a Determinant of Foreign Policy: John F. Kennedy's Operational Code," Southern California, 1979.

363. Usowski, Peter Stanley, "John F. Kennedy and the Central Intelligence Agency: Policy and Intelligence," George Washington, 1987.

Cuban Missile Crisis

364. Allison, Graham Tillett, Jr. "Policy, Process, and Politics: Conceptual Models and the Cuban Missile Crisis," Harvard, 1968.

365. Benjamin, Charles Michael. "Developing a Game/Decision Theoretic Approach to Comparative Foreign Policy Analysis: Some Cases in Recent American Foreign Policy," Southern California, 1981.

366. Bostdorff, Denise Marie. "The Contemporary Presidency and the Rhetoric of Promoted Crisis," Purdue, 1987.

367. Close, Patricia Margaret. "International Crises: An Analytical and Empirical Application of the Principle of Uncertainty," Carleton, 1978.

368. Halper, Thomas. "Appearance and Reality in True American Foreign Policy Crises," Vanderbilt, 1970.

369. Hoagland, Steven William. "Operational Codes and International Crises: The Berlin Wall and Cuban Missile Cases," Arizona State, 1978.

370. Layson, Walter Wells. "The Political and Strategic Aspects of the 1962 Cuban Crisis," Virginia, 1969.

371. Medland, William James. "The American-Soviet Nuclear Confrontation of 1962: An Historiographical Account of the Cuban Missile Crisis," Ball State, 1980.

372. Merchant, Jerrold Jackson. "Kennedy-Krushchev Strategies of Persuasion During the Cuban Missile Crisis," Southern California, 1971.

373. Parrent, Allan Mitchell. "The Responsible Use of Power: The Cuban Missile Crisis in Christian Perspective," Duke, 1969.

374. Renz, Mary Ann. "An Analysis of Argumentative Form and Negotiating Strategy in Three United Nations Security Council Debates," Wayne State, 1977.

375. Rimkus, Raymond Alston. "The Cuban Missile Crisis: A Decision-Making Analysis of the Quarantine Policy with Special Emphasis upon the Implication for Decision-Making Theory," Oklahoma, 1972.

376. Rogers, John Philip. "The Crisis Bargaining Code Model: The Influence of Cognitive Beliefs and Processes on US Policy-Making During Crises," Texas, 1986.

377. Ross, Bernard Harvey. "American Government in Crisis: An Analysis of the Executive Branch of Government During the Cuban Missile Crisis," New York, 1971.

378. Sandman, Joshua Harry. "The Cuban Missile Crisis: Developing a Prescriptive Model for Handling Nuclear Age Crisis," New York, 1978.

379. Shawky, A.G.M. "Stereotyped Images and International Crisis Communication: The Way Decision-Makers Define Situations in Foreign Affairs," London, 1987.

380. Skillern, William Gustaf. "An Analysis of the Decision-Making Process in the Cuban Missile Crisis," Idaho, 1971.

381. Trotter, Richard G. "The Cuban Missile Crisis: An Analysis of Policy Formulation in Terms of Current Decision Making Theory," Pennsylvania, 1970.

382. Wolbers, H.L. "On Some Aspects of the Communication of Intentions in Three Great Power Crises: The Outbreak of the Korean War, the Chinese Intervention in Korea, and the Cuban Missile Crisis," Oxford, 1975.

See also No. 416.

Cuba, the United States and Sugar

383. Abou-Bakr, Ahmed D. "The United States Sugar Position in the World Sugar Economy," Washington State, 1976.

384. Bates, Thomas Hobson. "The World Sugar Economy and United States Supply Policy," California, Berkeley, 1966.

385. Heston, Thomas Janney. "Sweet Subsidy: The Economic and Diplomatic Effects of the US Sugar Acts – 1934-1974," Case Western Reserve, 1975.

386. Markel, Robert Thomas. "The Politics of Sugar in the US Domestic and Foreign Affairs," Notre Dame, 1975.

387. Wolf, Harold Arthur. "The United States Sugar Policy and Its Impact Upon Cuba: A Re-Appraisal." Michigan, 1958.

388. Wright, Stephen John. "Cuba, Sugar and the United States: Diplomatic and Economic Relations During the Administration of Ramón Grau San Martín, 1944-1948," Pennsylvania State, 1983.

See also No. 57.

Puerto Rico and Cuba

389. Ward, Ana Mercedes R. "The Impact of the Cuban Revolution on the Political Status of Puerto Rico, 1959," Tulane, 1981.

390. White, Byron. "Cuba and Puerto Rico: A Case Study in Comparative Economic Development Policy," Texas, 1959.

The United Nations and Cuba

391. Cornelius, William Grigsby. "Latin American Patterns of Voting in the United Nations," Columbia, 1956.

392. De Camp, William Schuyler. "The Latin American Group in a Changing United Nations, 1955-1965," Tulane, 1971.

Canada and Cuba

393. Boyer, Harold. "Canada and Cuba: A Study in International Relations," Simon Fraser, 1973.

394. Guy, James John. "Canada's External Relations with Latin America: Environment, Process and Prospects," Saint Louis, 1975.

Caribbean and Cuba

395. Wolf, Donna Marie. "The Caribbean People of Color and the Cuban Independence Movement," Pittsburgh, 1973.

Latin America and Cuba

General

396. Kessler, Francis P. "The Futility of O.A.S. Collective Security: The Ninth Meeting of Foreign Ministers (Washington, DC, 1964)," Notre Dame, 1972.

397. Kwan, Moon Sool. "The Organization of American States and the Cuban Challenge: An Analysis of the Inter-American System and the Meeting of Consultation of Ministers of Foreign Affairs," Claremont, 1970.

398. Léger, Love O. "The Inter-American Peace Committee: An Attempted Integrated Structure of Peace Keeping in the Inter-American System," Temple, 1974 [1959].

399. Pak, Byung Koo. "The Cuban Problem in the Organization of American States: A Model for Collective Decision-Making," Florida State, 1965.

Brazil and Cuba

400. Means, John Barkley. "The Brazilian Intellectual's Response to Castro's Cuba," Illinois, 1969.

401. Rosenbaum, H. Jon. "Brazil's Foreign Policy and Cuba, 1950-1956," Tufts, Fletcher School of Law and Diplomacy, 1968.

Central America and Cuba

See No. 35

Chile and Cuba

402. Wolpin, Miles David. "The Influence of the Cuban Revolution Upon Chilean Politics and Foreign Policy, 1959-1965," Columbia, 1968.

Mexico and Cuba

403. Childers, Howard Ray, Jr. "Response of an Established Latin American Revolution to the Cuban Revolution: Mexican Symbols and Foreign Policy," Washington, St.Louis, 1970.

404. Engel, James Franklin. "Mexican Reaction to United States Cuban Policy, 1959-1963," Virginia, 1964.

405. Graves, Raymond J. "Mexican Foreign Policy Toward Cuba and Its Impact on US-Mexican Relations, 1970-1982," University of Miami, 1985.

406. Smith, Arthur Kittredge, Jr. "Mexico and the Cuban Revolution: Foreign Policy-Making in Mexico Under President Adolfo López Mateos, 1958-1964," Cornell, 1970.

The Soviet Union and Cuba

407. Blasier, Stewart Cole. "The Cuban and Chilean Communist Parties, Instruments of Soviet Policy, 1935-1948," Columbia, 1955.

408. Boughton, George John. "Soviet-Cuban Relations: 1956-1962," Michigan State, 1972.

409. González, Edward. "The Cuban Revolution and the Soviet Union, 1959-1960," California, Los Angeles, 1966.

410. Hamburg, Roger Phillip. "The Soviet Union and Latin America, 1953-1963," Wisconsin, 1965.

411. Messmer, William Bruce. "Soviet Agriculture and the Third World: A Case Study of Cuba," Ohio State, 1976.

412. Pope, Ronald Russell. "Soviet Foreign Affairs Specialists: An Evaluation of Their Direct and Indirect Impact on Soviet Foreign Policy Decision-Making Based on Their Analysis of Cuba, 1958-1961 and Chile, 1969-1973," Pennsylvania, 1975.

413. Rhoades, Margaret Mahaney. "Political Socialization in Cuba," Georgetown, 1973.

414. Robbins, Merritt Wesley. "Cuban-Soviet Relations, 1963-1968: An Asymmetrical Alliance Regime and the Politics of International Communist Gamesmanship," Harvard, 1978.

415. Schulz, Donald Edward. "The Cuban Revolution and the Soviet Union," Ohio State, 1977.

416. Selesnick, Herbert Lawrence. "The Diffusion of Crisis Information: A Computer Simulation of Soviet Mass Media Exposure during the Cuban and the Aftermath of President Kennedy's Assassination," Massachusetts Institute of Technology, 1970.

417. Shearman, Peter John. "Cuba: Soviet Surrogate or Maverick Ally?," Kansas, 1987.

See also Nos. 321, 866.

The Middle East and Cuba

418. Fernández, Damian J. "Cuba's Foreign Policy in the Middle East: 1959-1985," University of Miami, 1986.

Africa and Cuba

419. Abudu, Paul Bia. "Cuban Policy Toward Africa and African Responses 1959-1976," Howard, 1982.

420. Carle, Christophe Philippe Henry. "Cuba and Israel in Sub-Saharan Africa Since the 1950s: The Foreign Policies of Dependent States," Cambridge, 1987.

421. Singer, Eric. "The Effects of Leader Orientation and the External Environment on African Foreign Policy Behavior," Ohio State, 1986.

See also No. 875.

China and Cuba

422. Ratliff, William Elmore. "The Chinese Communist Domestic United Front and Its Application to Latin America," Washington, Seattle, 1974 [The People's Socialist Party of Cuba, 1959-1960].

Political Economy

See Nos. 69, 324, 896.

Political Geography

423. Fagon, Donald O'Connor. "The Geopolitics of the Caribbean Sea and Its Adjacent Lands," [Catholic, 1973].

See also No. 138.

Political Sociology

424. Allabar, Anton Laurence. "The Political Sociology of Colonial Underdevelopment: The Cuban Bourgeoisie as the Bitter-Sweet Taste of Sugar," Toronto, 1982.

425. Wickham-Crawley, Timothy Patrick. "A Sociological Analysis of Latin American Guerrilla Movements, 1956-1970," Cornell, 1981.

See also No. 298, 309, 815.

Cuban Americans and Politics in the United States

426. Nelson, Dale Cory. "Ethnicity and Political Participation in New York City: A Theoretical and Empirical Analysis," Columbia, 1977.

427. O'Leary, Thomas James. "Cubans in Exile: Political Attitudes and Political Participation," Stanford, 1967.

428. Quintanales, Mirtha Natacha. "The Political Radicalization of Cuban Youth in Exile: A Study of Identity Change in Bicultural Context," Ohio State, 1987.

429. Salces, Luis Mario. "Spanish American Politics in Chicago," Northwestern, 1978.

430. Stowers, Genie N.L. "Ethnic Political Development and Impact on Urban Policy: The Crucial Case of Cubans in Miami," Florida State, 1987.

431. Subervi Vélez, Federico Antonio. "Hispanics, the Mass Media, and Politics: Assimilation Versus Pluralism," Wisconsin, 1984 [Chicago].

432. Torres, Maria de los Angeles. "From Exiles to Minorities: The Politics of the Cuban Community in the United States," Michigan, 1986.

433. Wong, Francisco Ramundo. "The Political Behavior of Cuban Migrants," Michigan, 1974.

See also No. 119.

LANGUAGE

434. Baird, Keith Ethelbert. "A Critical Annotated Bibliography of African Linguistic Continuities in the Spanish Speaking Americas," The Union for Experimenting Colleges and Universities, 1982.

435. Barker, Gabriel. "A Functional-National Grammar of Some Aspects of Miami Cuban Spanish," Florida State, 1989.

436. Bjarkman, Peter Christian. 'Natural Phonology and Loanword Phonology (with Selected Examples from Miami Cuban Spanish," Florida, 1976.

437. Castellanos, Isabel Mercedes. "The Use of Language in Afro-Cuban Religion," Georgetown, 1977.

438. Fails, Willis Clark. "An Analysis of the Consonantal Phonemes of the Educated Norm of Havana," Texas, 1984.

439. Guitart, Jorge Miguel. "Markedness and a Cuban Dialect of Spanish," Georgetown, 1973.

440. Hammond, Robert Matthew. "Some Theoretical Implications from Rapid Speech Phonemes in Miami-Cuban Spanish," Florida, 1976.

441. Jacobs, Roderick Arnold. "Syntactic Change: A Cuban (Uto-Aztecan) Case Study," California, San Diego, 1972.

442. Lamb, Anthony J. "A Phonological Study of the Spanish of Havana, Cuba," Kansas, 1968.

443. MacDonald, Marguerite Goodrich. "Cuban-American English: The Second Generation in Miami," Florida, 1985.

444. Moya, Sharon Staggs. "Visual and Aural Monitoring Word Processing, and Voice Synthesization: Four Case Studies of Adult Non-English Language Background Writers," Florida, 1987.

445. Nieves, Enrique. "An Introductory Study of New York City Spanish Dialectology," Columbia, 1975 [Puerto Rican and Cuban].

446. Olarte, Gerardo. "Acquisition of Spanish Morphemes by Monolingual Monocultural Spanish-Speaking Children," Florida, 1985.

447. Orange, John Alexander, Jr. "Reflexive Constructions and Clitic Pronouns in Havana Spanish," Texas, 1981.

448. Radencich, Marguerite Cogorno. "The Role of Vocabulary in the Metaphysical Processing of Fluent and Less Fluent Users of English," University of Miami, 1983.

449. Rey, Alberto. "A Study of the Attitudinal Effect of a Spanish Accent on Blacks and Whites of South Florida," Georgetown, 1974.

450. Santiago, Bessie Norma. "Oral-Aural Communication Skills in English Among Adult Immigrants and Exiles." Michigan, 1980.

451. Sosa, Francisco. 'Sistema Fonologico del Español Hablado en Cuba: Su Posición dentro del Marco de la Lenguas, Criollas," Yale, 1974.

452. Stone, Gregory Bee. "Analysis of the Usage of Verbal Periphrases with the Gerund in the Educational Speech of Havana," Texas, 1980.

453. Vallejo Claros, Bernardo. "La Distribución y Estratificación de /r/à/Y/s/ en el Español Cubano," Texas, 1970.

LITERATURE

General

454. Badaracco, Claire M. "'The Cuba Journal' of Sophia Peabody Hawthorne, Volume I: Edited from the Manuscript with an Introduction," Rutgers, 1978.

455. Benz, Stephen Lee. "Graham Greene on Latin America: Non-fiction and Narrative Art," New Mexico, 1989.

456. Boydston, Jo Ann Harrison. "The Cuban Novel: A Study of Its Range and Characteristics," Columbia, 1950.

457. Bufill, José Angel. "Los Amigos Cubanos de Alfonso Reyes (un Dilogo Ennoblecido por la Cultura)," George Washington, 1986.

458. Burgos, Fernando. "El Concepto de Modernidad en el Novela Hispanoamericana," Florida, 1981.

459. Capellán, Angel. "Hemingway and the Hispanic World," New York, 1977.

460. Favi, Jeane D. "Chateaubriand's Influence Upon the Literature of Spain and Spanish-America," Northwestern, 1948.

461. Fernández Valledor, Roberto. "Identitad Nacional y Sociedad en la Ensayistica Cubana y Puertorriqueño (1920-1940), Mañach, Marinello, Pedreira y Blanco," Puerto Rico, 1986.

462. Frenk, S.F. "Carlos Fuentes and the Latin American 'Boom'," Cambridge, 1989.

463. García de Aldridge, Adriana. "De la Teoría a la Practica en la Novela Historica Hispanoamericana," Illinois, 1972.

464. Goodyear, Russell Howard. "A Critical Anthology of Contemporary Cuban Short Stories in Translation," Arkansas, 1978.

465. Hollingsworth, Charles. "The Development of Literary Theory in Cuba, 1959-1968," California, Berkeley, 1972.

466. Johnson, Maribel Dicker. "Thematic and Stylistic Development in Three Contemporary Cuban Novels," Colorado, 1984 [Alejo Carpenter, José Lezama Lima, Guillermo Cabrera Infante].

467. Johnson, Phillip. "Scenes of the City: The Urban Dilemma in the Contemporary Spanish American Novel," Utah, 1976.

468. Jones, Lewis P. "Carolinians and Cubans: The Elliots and Gonzales, Their Work and Their Writings," North Carolina, 1952.

469. Kapcia, A.M. "Changes and Developments in Cuban Literature Since the 1959 Revolution," London, 1980.

470. Lanning, Carmen Nadine. "The *Ambiente* of Five Latin American Novels by Graham Greene," Texas A & M, 1986.

471. La Russe, Evelyn Figueroa. "Modalidades Testemoniales y su Carnavalización en Cuba," Massachusetts, 1983 [Reynoldo Arenas, Miguel Barnet, Reneé Méndez Capote, Cintio Vitier].

472. Orrantia, Dagoberto. "The Situation of the Narrator as a Formal Principle in Four Representative Works of the Spanish-American New Novel," Illinois, 1977.

473. Ortúzar Young, Ada. "Tres Representaciones Literarias de la Urda Política Cubana," New York, 1979 [Carlos Loveiro, José Antonio Ramos, Luis Felipe Rodríguez].

474. Rostagno, Irene. "Fifty Years of Looking South: The Promotion and Reception of Latin American Literature in the U.S.," Texas, 1984.

475. Simpson, Amelia Stewart. "Social and Literary Expression in Latin American Detective Fiction," Texas, 1986.

476. Stewart, Janet Louise Beckwith. "The Concept of 'Lyrical Novel' as Seen in Three Spanish-American Novels," Texas, 1979.

See also Nos. 872, 879, 900.

History of Cuban Literature

477. Bortolussi, Marisa. "El Cuento Infantil en Cuba Antes y Después de la Revolución de 1959: Estatuto Teórico y Análisis Práctico," Laval, 1983.

478. Bresnahan, Roger James. "The Literature of the Spanish American War: An Anti-Imperialist Anthology," Massachusetts, 1974.

479. Casal, Lourdes. "Images of Cuban Society Among Pre- and Post-Revolutionary Novelists," New School for Social Research, 1975.

480. Casas, Nubya Celina. "Novela-Testimonia: Historia y Literatura," New York, 1981.

481. Colberg, Carmen Elias. "Esquema Histórico-Biogrfico de la Literatura Antillana Femenina en el Siglo XIX," North Carolina, 1989.

482. Figueroa, Armando. "Espacio y Mirada: Los Comienzos de la Narrativa en Cuba (1790-1850)," Columbia, 1990.

483. Kirby, Marjorie Tarleton. "A Literary History of the Cuban Short Story (1797-1959)," North Carolina, 1971.

484. Lax, Judith Heckelman. "Themes and Techniques in the Socially Oriented Cuban Novel: 1933-1952," Syracuse, 1961.

485. Méndez, Adriana Hilda. "The Historical Image in the Novel of the Cuban Revolution: Realism and Neobaroque." Cornell, 1979 [Spanish Text].

486. Méndez y Soto, Ernesto. "Panorama de la Novela Cubana de la Revolución (1959-1970)," Northwestern, 1973.

487. Smorkaloff, Pamela Maria. "Hacia una Historia Social de la Literatura Cubana de Siglo XX," New York, 1986.

488. Valdes, Bernardo José. "El Cuento Cubano en la República (1902-1959)," Illinois, 1974.

489. Véguez, Roberto Andrés. "Estudio Histórico-Crítico del Cuento Cubano Revolucionario," Wisconsin, 1975.

Literature of the Cuban in Exile

490. Fernández, Roberto G. "El Cuento Cubano del Exilio: Un Enfoque," Florida State, 1977.

491. Fernández Vásquez, Antonio Adolfo. "La Novela de la Revolución Cubano Escrita Fuera de Cuba: 1959-1975," Kentucky, 1978.

Folklore

492. Amor, Sister Rosa Teresa. "Afro-Cuban Folk Tales as Incorporated into the Literary Tradition of Cuba," Columbia, 1969.

493. Hansen, Terence Leslie. "The Types of Folktale in Cuba, Puerto Rico, the Dominican Republic, and Spanish South America," Stanford, 1952.

Revistas

494. Azize, Yamila. "Dos Revistas de la Decada del Treinta: La 'Revista Bernestre Cubana' y la Revista 'Ateneo Puertorriqueño'," Pennsylvania, 1980.

495. Barradás, Efrain. "La Revista 'Origenes' (1944-1956)," Princeton, 1978.

496. Ripoli, Carlos. "La Revista de Avance (1927-1930): Episodio de la Literatura Cubana," New York, 1964.

497. Sánchez-Eppler, Benigno. "Periodical Salvation of Circumstance: 'Cruz y Raya' (Madrid, 1933-36), 'Orígenes' (La Habana, 1944-56), and the Formation of Intellectual Communities," Johns Hopkins, 1988.

498. Zimmerman, Irene. "Latin American Periodicals of the Mid-Twentieth Century as Source Material for Research

in the Humanities and the Social Sciences," Michigan, 1956.

See also Nos. 881, 892.

Individual Authors

Alonso, Dora

499. Shea, Maureen Elisabeth. "Latin American Women Writers and the Growing Potential of Political Consciousness," Arizona, 1987.

Arenas, Reinaldo

500. Alvarado, Ela E. "Reinaldo Arenas y la Modernidad: Tradición y Ruptura," Wayne State, 1990.

501. Ocasio, Rafael. "La Narrativa de Reinaldo Arenas en el Contexto de la Revolución Cubana," Kentucky, 1987.

502. Rodríguez, Alicia Leonides. "Literature and Society: Three Novels by Reinaldo Arenas, 'Celestina antes del Alba', 'El Palacio de las Blanquisímas Mofetas' y 'Otra Vez el Mer'," Florida, 1987.

503. Rozencvaig, Perla. "The Fictionalization of History in Three Novels of Reinaldo Arenas," Columbia, 1983.

504. Soto, Francisco. "Reinaldo Arenas: Tradition and Similarity," New York, 1988.

505. Stewart, Janet Louise Beckwith. "The Concept of 'Lyrical Novel' as Seen in Three Spanish-American Novels," Texas, 1979.

506. Valero, Roberto. "Humor y Desolación en la Obra de *Reinaldo Arenas*," Georgetown, 1988.

See also No. 471.

Arrufat, Anton

507. Chiarella, Martha Betancourt. "El Carácter Agónico de los Personajes en las Obras Dramáticas de Anton Arrufat," Iowa, 1982.

Baeza Flores, Alberto

See No. 655.

Barnet, Miguel

508. Duchesne, Juan Ramón. "Testimonial Narratives in Latin America: Five Studies," SUNY, Stony Brook, 1984.

509. Sklodowska, Elzbieta. "La Visión de la Gente sin Historia en las Novelas Testimoniales de Miguel Barnet," Washington, St. Louis, 1983.

510. Vera León, Antonio S. "Testimonios Reescrituras. La Narrativa de Miguel Barnet," Princeton, 1987.

See also No. 471.

Benítez Rojo, Antonio

See No. 625.

Blanchot, Maurice

See No. 617.

Bobadilla, Emilio

511. Ledesma de los Reyes, Pedro Pablo. "Spanish Civilization in the Works of Emilio Bobadilla," Columbia, 1975.

Boti, Regino E.

512. De la Suarée, Octavio, Jr. "La Obra Literaria de Regino E. Boti," CUNY, 1976.

Cabrera Infante, Guillermo

513. Carpenter, Jane French. "The Ontological Prison: Paradoxes of Perception in the Contemporary Latin American Novel," Cornell, 1975.

514. Feal, Rosemary Geisdorfer. "Autobiography and Fiction: Cabrera Infante's 'La Habana Para el Infante Difunto' and Vargas Llosa's 'La Tia Julia y el Escribidor'," SUNY, Buffalo, 1984.

515. Ferguson, Theresa Pokrivnak. "Sustained Game Metaphors in Contemporary Novel: The Game is Life," Kansas, 1985.

516. García Serrano, Ma Victoria. "Writing and Orality in 'Tres Tristes Tigres'," Wisconsin, 1987 [Spanish Text].

517. Hernández Lima, Dinorah. "Versiones y Re-versiones Historicas en la obra de Guillermo Cabrera Infante," Maryland, 1983.

518. Jiménez Sánchez, Reynaldo Luis. "Guillermo Cabrera Infante y 'Tres Tristes Tigres'," Illinois, 1974.

519. Magnarelli, Sharon Dishaw. "The First Person in the Modern Spanish-American Novel," Cornell, 1975.

520. Merrim, Stephanie. "Logos and the Word; the Role of Language in 'Grande Sertao,' 'Veredas,' and 'Tres Tristes Tigres,'" Yale, 1978.

521. Mickelsen, Vicki Gillespie, "Games Novelists Play: Technical Experiments in 'La Muerte de Artemio Cruz'," 'La Casa Verde', 'Tres Tristes Tigres,' and 'Rayuela'," Indiana, 1974.

522. Nelson, Ardis Lorraine. "Characterization and Menippean Satire in the Major Works of Guillermo Cabrera Infante," Indiana, 1980.

523. Older, Dora Váquez. "El Juego Contradictorio en Cabrera Infante," Brown, 1977.

524. Retford, Lynne-Marie. "Anti-Mimesis, Language and Literature: A Study in Julio Cortazar's 'Rayuela,' Guillermo Cabrera Infante's 'Tres Tristes Tigres', José Donoso's 'El Obsceno Pjaro de la Noche', Alain-Fournier's 'Le Grand Meaulnes' and Julien Gracq's 'Au Chateau D'argol'," Oregon, 1984.

525. Siemens, William Lee, "Guillermo Cabrera Infante: Language and Creativity." Kansas, 1971.

526. Stone, Barbara Anne Aszman. "Space in Three Contemporary Spanish American Novels," Texas, 1986. ["Tres Tristes Tigres"]

See also Nos. 12, 466, 558, 724, 885.

Cardoso, Onelio Jorge

527. Pavlakis, Efthymia P. "Onelio Jorge Cardoso: Cuentero para Niños y Adultos," New York, 1988.

Carpentier Alejo

528. Adams, Michael Ian. "Alienation in Selected Works of Three Contemporary Spanish-American Authors," Texas, 1972.

529. Addis, Mary Kathryn. "The Novel of the Dictator: History as Narrative Form," California, San Diego, 1984.

530. Alexander, Roberta May. "The Fictional Portrayal of Popular Movements," California, San Diego, 1979.

531. Alonso, Juan Manuel. "The Search for Identity in Alejo Carpentier's Contemporary Urban Novels; An Analysis of 'Los Pasos Perdidos' and 'El Acoso'," Brown, 1967.

532. Angulo, Mauria Elena. "'Realismo Maravilloso' and Social Context in Five Modern Latin American Novels," California, Berkeley, 1989.

533. Assardo, Maurice Roberto. "La Técnica Narrativa en la Obra de Alejo Carpentier: Enfasis: El Tiempo," California, Los Angeles, 1968.

534. Baker, Armand Fred. "El Tiempo en la Novela Hispanoamericana: Un Estudio del Concepto del Tiempo en Siete Novelas Representativas," Iowa, 1967.

535. Barroso, Juan, VIII. "Realismo Mágico y 'Lo Real Maravilloso' en 'El Reino de Este Mundo' y 'El Siglo de las Luces'," Louisiana State, 1975.

536. Baxter, J.R. "A Certain Unity of Purpose: Alejo Carpentier and His Novel 'La Consagracíon de la Primavera'," Aberdeen, 1982.

537. Beltrán Vocal, María Antonia. "Temas y Técnicas Narratives en la Novela Española e Hispanoamericana Contemporánea," California, Riverside, 1985.

538. Budig, Valerie Jean. "The Self-Reflexive Historical Novel," Alejo Carpentier and Claude Simon," Oregon, 1989.

539. Bush, Roland Edward. "The Art of *La Fuga*: Mythic and Musical Modes in Relation to the Theme of Identity in Alejo Carpentier's 'Los Pasos Perdidos'," Southern California, 1981.

540. Cano, Carlos José. "Tres Momentos Significativos en la Novelística Hispanoamericana Contempornea," Indiana, 1973.

541. Captain-Hidalgo, Yvonne. "The Realm of Possible Realities: A Comparative Analysis of Selected Novels by Alejo Carpentier and Manuel Zapata Olivella," Stanford, 1984.

542. Carter-Burke, Sheila Nani. "A Feeling for Music: Carpentier's 'El reino de este mundo,' 'Los paises perdidos' and 'El siglo de las luces,'" California, Davis, 1989.

543. Castillo, Eduardo del. "La Crítica de la Fricción Hispanoamericana (1942-1972)," Missouri, 1974.

544. Charles, Asselin. "The Limits of Marvelous Realism: Alejo Carpentier, Jacques Stephen Alexis, and Amos Tutuola," Pennsylvania State, 1989.

545. Chase, Ada Solano. "Correlación entre Algunos Procedimentos Estilisticos y la Temtica en la Ficción Extensa de Alejo Carpentier hasta 'El Siglo De Los Luces'," Oklahoma, 1976.

546. Cheuse, Alan. "Memories of the Future: A Critical Biography of Alejo Carpentier," Rutgers, 1974.

547. Colavita, Federica Domínguez. "El Sentido de la Historia en la Obra de Alejo Carpentier," Washington, St. Louis, 1974.

548. Díaz, Nancy Gray. "Metamorphosis from Human to Animal Form in Five Modern Latin American Narratives," Rutgers, 1984.

549. Díaz, Ramón. "El Simbolismo en Cuatro Obras de Alejo Carpentier," California, Los Angeles, 1979.

550. Drake, Sandra Elizabeth. "The Uses of History in the Caribbean Novel," Stanford, 1977.

551. Fernández, Ricardo R. "La Novelistica de Alejo Carpentier," Princeton, 1970.

552. Fernández Rubio, Ramón. "El Eco y Otros Recursos Estilisticos en la Novelistica de Alejo Carpentier," Georgia, 1979.

553. Floyd, Jo Ann. "The Journey Home: The Intellectual's Search for Identity in Five Spanish-American Novels," Teachers College, Columbia, 1979.

554. García Castro, Ramón F.J. "Perspectivas Temporales en la Obra de Alejo Carpentier," Pennsylvania, 1972.

555. Gerhold, Kathryn Marie. "The Aesthetic Use of the Epigraph in the Works of Alejo Carpentier," Northwestern, 1981.

556. González, Eduardo Gumersindo. "El Tiempo del Hombre: Huella y Labor de Origen en Cuatro Obras de Alejo Carpentier," Indiana, 1975.

557. Green, George K. "The Early Writings of Alejo Carpentier (1923-1949)," Columbia, 1976.

558. Hayworth, Karen Lyn Getty. "Language and Technique in *Tres Tristes Tigres* and *El Recurso del Método*," Texas, 1979.

559. Herrera, Armando Antonio. "Love and Death in the Novels of Alejo Carpentier," [Spanish Text], Florida State, 1981.

560. Hidalgo, Jorge. "El Tiempo y Las Formas en Tres Obras de Alejo Carpentier," Emory, 1974.

561. Jaguaribe de Mattos, Beatriz. "The Totalizing Narrative: Four Latin American Case Studies," Stanford, 1986 [*El Siglo de las Luces*].

562. Janney, Frank Fay. "The Way of Return: Regression in the Early Works of Alejo Carpentier," Harvard, 1972.

563. Jones, Julie. "The Representation of Paris in Spanish-American Fiction," Tulane, 1989.

564. Kapschutschenko, Ludmila. "El Laberinto en la Narrativa Hispanoamericana Contemporánea," Pennsylvania, 1974.

565. Kilmer-Tchalekian, Mary Alice. "Synthesis as Process and Vision in *El Siglo De Las Luces* and *Cien Años de Soledad*," Texas, 1974.

566. Kolodney, Bette Krupenin. "Técnicas Suprarrealistas en Obras Escogidas de Ficción Hispanoamericana Contempornea," Connecticut, 1975.

567. Langowski, Gerald John. "Surrealism in Spanish American Fiction," Wisconsin, 1973.

568. Lester, Margaret Nancy. "The Function of the Journey-and-Return Story in Representative Latin American Novels," Colorado, 1973 [*Los Pasos Perdidos*].

569. Mandelbaum, Ann. "El Perfil de la Cultura en la Obra de Alejo Carpentier," Wayne State, 1986.

570. Martin, Claire Emilie. "Alejo Carpentier y las Crónicas de Indias: Orígenes de una Escritura Americana," Yale, 1988.

571. Matibag, Eugenio Dulog. "The Sleep of Reason: Alejo Carpentier and the Crisis of Latin American Modernity," California, Irvine, 1986.

572. McGregor, J.W. "Man and Society: The Motion of Responsibility in the Novels of Alejo Carpentier," St. Andrews, 1982.

573. Mocega González, Esther P. "El Pasado Histórico en la Novelistica de Alejo Carpentier," Chicago, 1973.

574. Mojica, Rafael Humberto. "Prolegomenos a la Materia Americana," Colorado, 1989.

575. Montero, Janina. "La Perspectiva Histórica en Augusto Roa Bastos, Alejo Carpentier and Gabriel García Márquez," Pennsylvania, 1973.

576. Mueller Bergh, Klaus. "La Prosa Narrativa de Alejo Carpentier en 'Los Pasos Perdidos'," Yale, 1966.

577. Navarro, M.H. "Aspects of Power and History in the Dictator Novels by Alejo Carpentier, Augusto Roa Bastos and Gabriel García Márquez," London, 1985.

578. Ortiz, Nora Myares. "Alejo Carpentier: Un Estudio de 'Los Pasos Perdidos'," Florida State, 1978.

579. Pacheco, José Ignacio. "La Obra Narrativa de Alejo Carpentier," California, Riverside, 1973.

580. Peavler, Terry Joe. "The Development of Alejo Carpentier's Narrative Technique," California, Berkeley, 1973.

581. Pérez Reilly, Elizabeth Kranz. "'Lo Real Maravilloso' in the Prose Fiction of Alejo Carpentier: A Critical Study," Vanderbilt, 1975.

582. Piffault Hafsi, Joelle Laurence. "La Consagración de la Primavera: Hacía una Novela en la Forma de Ballet," Boston University, 1983.

583. Ribe, Enriqueta. "La Production de sens implicite dans 'El Recurso del Metodo' d'Alejo Carpentier," Montreál, 1986.

584. Riveros Schafer, Enrique. "Flights from the Polis: A Study of Joseph Conrad's 'Heart of Darkness', José Eustasio Rivers 'La Voragine', Graham Greene's 'A Burnt Out Case' and Alejo Carpentier's 'Los Pasos Perdidos'," California, San Diego, 1982.

585. Rodríguez, Ileana. "La Política de la Producción Literaria en Dos de las Principales Novelas de Carpentier," California, San Diego, 1976.

586. Rojas Paiewonsky, Lourdes. "Dos Formas Complementarias de Mitificación y Desmitificación de la Mujer en la Primera Generación Surrealista: 'La Creación' de Agustin Yañez y 'Los Pasos Perdidos" de Alejo Carpentier," SUNY, Stony Brook, 1985.

587. Salazar, Carol Lacy. "La Cosmovisíon Primitiva del Narrador Magicorrealista," Arizona, 1984.

588. Saldivar, José David. "Claiming the Americas: Contemporary Third World Literature," Stanford, 1983.

589. Sánchez, Marta Ester. "Three Latin American Novelists in Search of *Lo Americano*: A Productive Failure," California, San Diego, 1977.

590. Sánchez, Napoleón Neptali. "El Surrealismo: Fermento Transformador en la Obra Novelística de Alejo Carpentier," Massachusetts, 1977.

591. Skinner, Eugene Raymond. "Archetypal Patterns in Four Novels of Alejo Carpentier," Kansas, 1969.

592. Sokoloff, Naomi Beryl. "Spatial Form in the Social Novel: John Dos Passos, Alejo Carpentier, and S.Y. Agnon," Princeton, 1980.

593. Soto Borges, Valentín. "The Historical Portrayal in Alejo Carpentier," Stanford, 1986.

594. Soto Feliú, Román Evaristo. "The Hero in Six Spanish-American Novels: A Semiotic Approach," Catholic, 1987.

595. St. Omer, Garth. "The Colonial Novel: Studies in the Novels of Albert Camus, V.S. Naipaul, and Alejo Carpentier," Princeton, 1975.

596. Thompson, Mercedes Arissó. "La Imagen del Caudillo en la Novela Hispanoamericana Contempornea." Colorado, 1977.

597. Torres Rosado, Santos. "Visión de la Mujer en las Novelas de Alejo Carpentier," California, Los Angeles, 1990.

598. Valiela, Isabel. "La Función del Lenguaje en 'El Siglo de Las Luces' de Alejo Carpentier," Duke, 1977.

599. Webb, Barbara J. "Myth and History in the Novels of Alejo Carpentier and Wilson Harris: Theories of Cultural Transformation," New York, 1985.

600. Worth, Fabienne Andre. "Historical Modes of Narration in Four Twentieth Century Novels: Marcel Proust's 'A la recherche du temps perdu,' Alejo Carpentier's 'Los Pasos

Perdidos,' Virginia Woolf's 'Between the Acts,' Gunter Grass's 'Die Blechtrommel'," North Carolina, 1979.

601. Zabala, Mercedes. "Alejo Carpentier: Un Mundo en Metamorfosis (Estudio Estilístico)," Columbia, 1971.

See also Nos. 443, 676-678, 882, 900.

Cid, José

602. Davis, Michele Star. "Proyecciónes Estilísticas en los Personajes Femeninos de José Cid," Purdue, 1979.

de Carrión, Miguel

603. González, Mirza L. "La Novela y el Cuento Psicológicos de Miguel de Carrión," Northwestern, 1974.

Delmonte y Aponte, Domingo

604. Karras, Bill James. "The Literary Life of Domingo Delmonte y Aponte," Colorado, 1969.

Díaz, Jésus

605. Cachán, Manuel. "El Discurso Narrativo del Caribe Hispano: Una Perspectiva del Cuento (1960-1970)," Tulane, 1988.

Fuentes, Norberto

See No. 661.

Gómez de Avellaneda, Gertrudis

606. Judicini, Joseph Victor. "Revision in Characterization and Structure in the Plays of Gertrudis Gómez de Avellaneda," California, Berkeley, 1986.

607. Lazcano, Antonio María. "Gertrudis Gómez de Avellaneda: Ideas About Cuban Society of Her Times in Her Prose," Minnesota, 1977.

608. Moore, Suzanne Shelton. "Themes and Characterization in the Dramatic Works of Gertrudis Gomez de Avellaneda," Tulane, 1976.

609. Ortíz Cardona, Evelyn. "La Posición de la Mujer en la Obra de Gertrudis Gómez de Avellaneda," Puerto Rico, 1986.

610. Piñera, Estela A. "The Romántic Theater of Gertrudis Gómez de Avellaneda," New York, 1974.

611. Reed, Miriam Asenjo. "Las Protagonistas Romnticas en las Novelas de Gertrudis Gómez de Avellaneda," North Carolina, 1989.

See also Nos. 694, 695, 748.

Greimas, Algirdas

See No. 672.

Heras León, Eduardo

See No. 661.

Hernández Cata, Alfonso

612. Febles, Jorge Manuel. "Modalidades del Cuento en la Obra de Alfonso Hernández Cata," Iowa, 1975.

613. González, Anisia M. "Las Novelas Cortas de Alfonso Hernández Cata," Florida State, 1970.

614. Gutiérrez de la Solana, Alberto. "Lino Novas Calvo y Alfonso Hernández Cata: Contraste de Vida y Obra," New York, 1967.

Leante, César

615. Luis, William. "César Leante: The Politics of Fiction," Cornell, 1980.

Lezama Lima, José (see Poetry also)

616. Borgman, Ruth Elizabeth. "El Lenguaje Literario en 'Paradiso' de José Lezama Lima," Universidad Nacional Autonoma de Mexico," 1982.

617. Bush, Andrew Keith. "Portals of Discovery: Maurice Blanchot, José Lezama Lima, Reinaldo Arenas," Yale, 1983.

618. Camacho Rivero de Gingerich, Alina Luisa. "La Cosmovision Poética de José Lezama Lima en 'Paradiso' y 'Oppiano Licario'," Pittsburgh, 1983.

619. Cruz, Arnaldo. "The Problematics of Origin in José Lezama Lima's 'Paradiso'," Stanford, 1984.

620. Fernández, Luis Francisco. "José Lezama Lima y la Crítica Anagórica," Illinois, 1975.

621. Gimbernat de González, Ester. "'Paradiso': Aventura Sigilosa de un Sistema Poético," Johns Hopkins, 1975.

622. Moreiras, Alberto. "Interpretación y Diferencia: Análisis de Estructuras Interpretativas," Georgia, 1987.

623. Rivera, Puro A. "Repercussion of the Baroque in José Lezama Lima's Narrative: The Short Stories and 'Paradiso'," California, San Diego, 1987 [Spanish Text].

624. Ulloa, Justo Celso. "La Narrativa de Lezama Lima y Sarduy: Entre la Imágen Visionaria y el Juego Verbal," Kentucky, 1973.

See also Nos. 698-704, 886.

Loveira, Carlos

625. Artalejo, Lucrecía. "La Mscara y el Marañon: La Identitad Nacional Cubana en el Narrativa de Cirilo Villaverde, Carlos Loveira y Antonio Benítez Rojo," Cornell, 1987.

626. Marqués, Sarah. "Arte y Sociedad en las Novelas de Carlos Loveira," New York, 1976.

627. Martínez, Miguel Angel. "Visión Cubana de Carlos Loveira," Northwestern, 1969.

See also No. 473.

Mañach, Jorge

628. Alvarez, Nicols Emilio. "La Obra Literaria de Jorge Mañach," California, Berkeley, 1973.

629. De La Torre, Amalia María V. "Jorge Mañach, Maestro del Ensayo," Indiana, 1975.

630. Martí, Jorge Luis. "El Periodismo Literario de Jorge Mañach," SUNY, Buffalo, 1970.

631. O'Cherony, Rosalyn Krantzler. "The Critical Essays of Jorge Mañach," Northwestern, 1970 [Portions of text in Spanish].

632. Riccio, Guy John. "Hispanidad and the Growth of National Identity in Contemporary Spanish-American Thought," Maryland, 1963.

633. Valdespino, Andrés Alberto. "Significación Literaria de Jorge Mañach," New York, 1968.

See also Nos. 461, 655.

Marinello, Juan

See No. 461.

Martí, José

634. Allen, David Harding, Jr. "Ariel and Caliban: The Turning Point (1870-1900)," California, Los Angeles, 1968.

635. Alonso, Luis Ricardo. "Hostos y Martí: Novelistas," Boston College, 1975.

636. Andino, Alberto. "España en la Obra de Martí," Columbia, 1971.

637. Ballon-A., José Carlos. "Cultural Autonomy: From Emerson to Martí," Stanford, 1981 [Spanish Text].

638. Brodermann, Ramón E. "El Pensamiento Literario de José Martí: Sus Mocedades," Florida State, 1972.

639. Corbitt, Roberta Day. "This Colossal Theater: The United States Interpreted by José Martí," Kentucky, 1956.

640. Fountain, Anne Owen. "José Martí and North American Authors," Columbia, 1973.

641. Gordon, Alan Martin. "Verb Creation in the Works of José Martí: Method and Function," Harvard, 1956.

642. Iduart, Andrés. "Martí Escritor." Columbia, 1944.

643. Knapp, Noemí Escandell. "Cuarenta Artículos Desconocidos de José Martí," Harvard, 1976.

644. Langhorst, Frederick Horst. "Three Latin Americans Look at US: The United States as Seen in the Essays of José Martí, José Enrique Rodó, and José Vasconcelos," Emory, 1975.

645. Mas, José L. "Perspectiva Ideológica de José Martí en Sus Crónicas sobre los Estados Unidos," California, Los Angeles, 1974.

646. Molina de Galindo, Isis. "La Modalidad Impresionista en la Obra de José Martí," California, Los Angeles, 1966.

647. Pericone, Catherine Lee. "A Study of Anti-Modernism," Tulane, 1973.

648. Quesada, Luis Manuel. "José Martí: Cuentos de *La Edad de Oro*. Edición Estudiantil con Introducción, Vocabulario y Notas," Florida State, 1968.

649. Ramos, Julio. "Contradiciones de la Modernización Literaria en América Latina: José Martí y la Crónica Modernista," Princeton, 1986.

650. Rivera Meléndez, Blanca Margarita. "Poetry and Machinery of Illusion: José Martí and the Poetics of Modernity," Cornell, 1990.

651. Rotker, Susana R. "José Martí: La Fundacción de una Nueva Escritura," Maryland, 1989.

652. Schulman, Ivan Albert. 'Symbolism and Color in the Works of José Martí," California, Los Angeles, 1959.

653. Sneary, Eugene Chester. "José Martí in Translation," Tulane, 1959.

654. Stark, Bernice Sutherland. "The Presence and Significance of the Indian in Modernism," Pittsburgh, 1970.

655. Sternlicht, Madeline. "Man or Myth: José Martí in the Biographies of Jorge Mañach, Alberto Baeza Flores, and Ezequiel Martínez Estrada," Columbia, 1976.

656. Suárez Franceschi, Arsenio. "América en Martí," Puerto Rico, 1987.

See also Nos. 192, 194, 196, 198, 705-709, 877.

Martínez Estrada, Ezequiel

See No. 655.

Méndez Capote Renée

See No. 471.

Meza y Suárez Inclan, Ramón

657. González Freixas, Manuel Alberto. "Sociedad y Tipos en las Novelas de Ramón Meza y Suárez Inclán," Florida, 1980.

Montenegro, Carlos

658. Pujols, Enrique J. "Carlos Montenegro: de la Biografía en la Narrativa," Rutgers, 1978.

Novas Calvo, Lino

659. Souza, Raymond Dale. "The Literary World of Lino Novas Calvo," Missouri, 1964.

See also No. 614.

Ortiz, Fernando

660. Barnett, Curtis Lincoln Everard, "Fernando Ortiz and the Literary Process," Columbia, 1986.

See also No. 725, 732.

Padilla, Herberto

661. Hernández Morelli, Rolando D'Abraldes. "Los Héroes Juzgados: La Vision Crítico-Paródica del Héroe, en Tres Obras Escritos en Cuba entre 1966 y 1970: *Condenados de Condado* de Norberto Fuentes, *Los Pasos en la Hierba* de Eduardo-Heras León y *En mi Jardín Pastan los Héroes* de Herberto Padilla," Temple, 1987.

See also No. 712, 743, 899.

Piñera, Virgilio

662. Aguilu de Murphy, Raquel. "The Dramatic Texts of Virgilio Piñera and the Latin American Absurdist Movement," Wisconsin, 1984 [Spanish Text].

663. López Ramírez, Tomás. "El Absurdo y la Condición Humana en la Narrativa de Virgílio Piñera," Syracuse, 1982.

664. Torres Robles, Carmen L. "Estrategias Humorísticas en la Cuentística de Virgilio Piñera," Rutgers, 1988.

See also No. 20.

Plácido (Gabriel de la Concepción Valdés)

665. Carruthers, Ben. "The Life Work and Death of Plácido," Illinois, 1941.

666. García, Enildo Albert. "Cuba en la Obra de Plácido (1809-1844): Analisis y Bibliografía Comentada," New York, 1982.

Ramos, José Antonio

667. McElroy, Onyria Herrera. "Nacionalismo en la Obra Literaria de José Antonio Ramos," Arizona, 1981.

See also No. 473.

Rodríguez, Luis Felipe

See No. 473

Sarduy, Severo

668. Incledon, John Scott. "The Fearful Sphere: Difference and Repetition in the Writing of Jorge Luis Borges, Julio Cortazar, and Severo Sarduy," SUNY, Binghamton, 1979.

669. Kushigian, Julia Alexis. "Three Versions of Orientalism in Contemporary Latin American Literature: Sarduy, Borges and Paz," Yale, 1984.

670. Montero, Oscar Julian. "The French Intertext of 'De Donde Son Los Cantantes,'" North Carolina, 1978.

See also No. 624.

Secadas, Eladio

671. De Lama, Sonia Gisela. "Les Estampas de Eladio Secadas Publicadas en 'Zig-Zag Libre'," Northwestern, 1973.

Triana, José

672. Fernández Fernández, Ramiro. "La Estética del Absurdo en los Textos Dramáticos de José Triana: Una Aplicación de la Semiotica Textual de Algirdas Greimas," Temple, 1985.

See also Nos. 16, 24.

Varona, Enrique José

673. Alba, Elio. "Enrique José Varona: Crítica y Creación Literaria," New York, 1974.

674. Martínez, Oscar. "Vida y Obras de Enrique Varona, Ensayista Cubano," Florida State, 1972.

Villaverde, Cintio

675. Farinas, Lucila. "Las Dos Versiones de Cecilia Valdés: Evolución Temático-Literaria," New York, 1979.

676. Karras, M. Elizabeth Tucker. "Tragedy and Illicit Love: A Study of the Incest Motif in Cecilia Valdés and Os Maias," Colorado, 1973.

677. Norman, Isabel Hernández. "La Novela Romantica de las Antilles," Yale, 1966 [Cecilia Valdés].

See also No. 625.

Vitier, Cintio

See No. 471, 714.

Poetry

General

678. Caccavale, Mirtha Galban. "Poesía Cubana de la Revolución 1959-1979: Historia y Política." Southern California, 1981.

679. Fraker, C.J. "The Development of Modernism in Spanish American Poetry," Harvard, 1931.

680. Godoy, Gustavo J. "La Generación Cubana de Poetas Posmodernistas," University of Miami, 1967.

681. Olivera, Otto H. "Lo Nacional en la Poesía Cubana, 1511-1898," Tulane, 1953.

See also No. 876.

Individual Poets

Acosta, Agustin

682. Fores, Aldo Ramón. "The Poetry of Agustín Acosta, 'National Poet of Cuba'," Minnesota, 1976.

Ballagas, Emilio

683. De la Torre, Rogelio Armando. "Emilio Ballagas, Poeta de su Tiempo." Indiana, 1974.

684. Rice, Argyll Pryor. "Emilio Ballagas: Poeta o Poesía," Yale, 1961.

See also Nos. 681, 686, 728, 730.

Benet y Castellón, Eduardo

685. Brower, Gary Layne. "The *Haiku* in Spanish American Poetry." Missouri, 1966.

Brull Caballero, Mariano

686. Collins, Maria Castellanos. "Brull, Florit, Ballagas y el Vanguardismo en Cuba," Kentucky, 1976.

687. Larraga, Ricardo. "Mariano Brull y la Poesía Pura en Cuba: Bibliografía y Evolución," New York, 1981.

688. Villar, Aurora María. "La Poesía de Mariano Brull," Indiana, 1981.

Cernuda, Luis

See No. 702.

Del Casal, Julian

689. Gómez Cortes, Quirino Francisco Rubén. "Julian Del Casal: The Man and His Poetry," Florida State, 1973.

690. Hernández Miyares, Julio E. "Julian Del Casal, Escritor," New York, 1972.

Fernández Retamar, Roberto

691. Bornstein, Miriam Mijalina. "Nueva Poesía Sociopolítica: La Expresión Hispana," Arizona, 1982.

692. Medina Valin, Niurka. "La Poesía Circumstancial de Roberto Fernández Retamar en su Contexto Histórico _ Cultural, 1948-1980." Southern California, 1987.

Florit, Eugenio

693. Strathdee, Katharine Elizabeth. "The Four Greek Elements in the Poetry of Eugenio Florit," California, Los Angeles, 1979.

See also no. 686.

Gómez de Avellaneda, Gertrudis

694. Rosello, Aurora Julia. "La Poesía Lírica de Gertrudis Gómez de Avellaneda," Southern California, 1973.

695. Vieira Branco, Maria Elena. "Gertrudis Gómez de Avellaneda in the Context of Nineteenth Century Spanish Lyric," Pennsylvania, 1990.

Heredia, José María

696. Díaz, Lomberto. "José María Heredia: Vida y Obra del Primer Romántico Hispanoamericano," Florida State, 1969.

697. Garcerán de Vall, Julio A. "Síntesis de Díctomia Libertad-Independencia en la Poesía de Heredia," SUNY, Albany, 1976.

Lezama Lima, José

698. Beaupied, Aida María. "Narciso Hermético: Sr. Juana Inés de la Cruz y José Lezama Lima," Yale, 1988.

699. Bertot, Lillian D. "Linguistic and Stylistic Approaches to the Poetry of José Lezama Lima," Florida, 1984 [Spanish text].

700. Collazo, Conrado. "La Poética de la Fragmentario de José Lezama Lima." SUNY, Stony Brook, 1984.

701. Cruz Alvarez, Félix L. "Los Poetas del Grupo de *Orígenes*," University of Miami, 1977.

702. Garrido Bassanini, Christine. "De Eros y Poética: Itinerarios de José Lezama Lima y Luis Cernuda," Purdue, 1987.

703. Lutz, Robyn Rothrock. "The Poetry of José Lezama Lima," Kansas, 1950.

704. Márquez, Enrique. "José Lezama Lima: Una Poética de la Figuración," University of Miami, 1979.

See also Nos. 616-624.

Martí, José

705. Capuano, Isaac. "El Desdoblamiento del 'yo' en la Poesía de José Martí, Miguel de Unamuno, Antonio Machado y Juan Ramón Jiménez," CUNY, 1976.

706. Hernández Chiroldes, Juan Alberto. "Análisis Crítico de los 'Versos Sencillos' de José Martí," Texas, 1978.

707. Rey Barreau, José Luis. "El Concepto de la Muerte en Cuatro Poetas Premodernistas," Kentucky, 1971.

708. Rivera, Blanca Margarita. "Poetry and Machinery of Illusion: José Martí and the Poetics of Modernity," Cornell, 1990.

709. Shuler, Esther Elise. "Poesía y Teorias Poéticas de José Martí (con especial referencia a su crítica de autores Norteamericanos)," Minnesota, 1947.

710. Wilson, Charles Kendall. "Imagery in the Poetry of José Martí," Illinois, 1975.

See also Nos. 634-656.

Martínez Villena Rubén

711. Yanes, Pedro Armando. "Rubén Martínez Villena: Conflictos entre Poesía y Política," New York, 1983.

Padilla, Herberto

712. Garabedian, Martha Ann. "Imagery and Experience in the Poetry of Oscar Hahn, José Emilio Pacheco and Herberto Padilla: A New Expression of Reality in Three Contemporary Spanish American Poets," Connecticut, 1984.

See also Nos. 661, 743.

Uhrbach, Carlos Prío and Federico

713. Fernández, Lilia. "El Mundo Poético de los Urbach," Northwestern, 1974.

Vitier, Cintio

714. García Marruz, Graciela. "La Obra Poética de Cintio Vitier," CUNY, 1982.

See also No. 471.

Black Literature and Poetry in Cuba

715. Barreda, Pedro Manuel. "La Caracterización del Protagonista Negra en la Novela Cubana," SUNY, Buffalo, 1969.

716. De Ruiz, María de Jésus Paez C. "El Tema de la Esclavitud en Novelas Representativas de la Literatura Cubana y Brasileña del Siglo XIX," Louisiana State, 1983.

717. García, Calixto. "El Negro en la Narrativa Cubana," CUNY, 1973.

718. Gordils, Janice Doris. "La Herencia Africana en la Literatura Cubana de Hoy," New York, 1976.

719. Hewitt, Julia Irene Cuervo. "Yoruba Presence in Contemporary Cuban Narrative," Vanderbilt, 1981 [Spanish text].

720. Olchyk, Marta K. "Historical Approach to Afro-Cuban Poetry," Texas Christian, 1972.

721. Williams, Claudette May. "Images of the Black and Mulatto Woman in Spanish Caribbean Poetry," Stanford, 1986.

See also Nos. 17, 19, 492.

Individual Authors

Cabrera, Lydia

722. Gutierrez, Mariela. "Los Cuentos Negros de Lydia Cabrera: Estudio Morfológico Esquemtico," Laval, 1985.

723. Soto, Sara. 'Magia de Historia en los 'Cuentos Negros', 'Por Que' y 'Ayapá' de Lydia Cabrera," New York, 1985.

Cabrera Infante, Guillermo

724. Hampton, Janet Jones. "The Image of the Black Woman in the Spanish-American Novel: A Study of Characterization in Selected Spanish-American Novels," Catholic, 1985.

See also Nos. 513-526.

Carpentier, Alejo

725. Jackson, Shirley Mae. "Temas Principales de la Novela Negrista Hispano-Americana en López Albíjar, Díaz Sánchez, Carpentier, Ortiz, y Zapata Olivella," George Washington, 1982.

726. Menéndez, Raymat Andrés. "Negritude e Identitad Nacional en la Narrativa de Alejo Carpentier," Yale, 1985.

727. Piedra, José. "The Afro-Cuban Esthetics of Alejo Carpentier," Yale, 1985.

See also Nos. 495-562

De Lima, Jorge

See No. 746.

Gómez de Avellaneda, Gertrudis

See No. 748.

Guillén, Nicolás

728. Boulware Miller, Patricia Kay. "Nature in Three 'Negrista' Poets: Nicols Guillén, Emilio Ballagas and Luis Palés Matos," California, Berkeley, 1978.

729. Boyd, Antonio Olliz. "The Concept of Black Esthetics as Seen in Selected Works of Three Latin American Writers: Machado de Assis, Nicolás Guillén and Adalberto Ortiz," Stanford, 1975.

730. Cartey, Wilfred George Onslow. "Three Antillean Poets: Emilio Ballagas, Luis Palés Matos, and Nicols Guillén: Literary Development of the Negro Theme in Relation to the Making of Modern Afro-Antillean Poetry and the Historic Evolution of the Negro," Columbia, 1975.

731. Castan Pontrelli, Mary. "The *Criollo* Poetry of Nicolas Guillén," Yale, 1958.

732. Catzaras, Marina. "El Negrismo en Cuba: Ortiz, Guillén, Carpentier," Pittsburgh, 1990.

733. Cobb, Martha K. "The Black Experience in the Poetry of Nicols Guillén, Jacques Roumain, Langston Hughes," Catholic, 1974.

734. Coin, Jeannette Bercovici. "Social Aspects of Black Poetry in Luis Palés Matos, Nicols Guillén, and Manuel Del Cabral," New York, 1976.

735. Davis, Stephanie Jo. "Development of Poetry Techniques in the Works of Nicols Guillén," Princeton, 1976.,

736. De García Barrio, Constance Sparrow. "The Black in Cuban Literature and the Poetry of Nicols Guillén, Pennsylvania, 1975.

CUBA, CUBANS, AND CUBAN-AMERICANS 75

737. Farrell, Joseph Richard. "Nicolás Guillén: Poet in Search of *Cubanidad*," Southern California, 1968.

738. Kubayanda, Josaphat Bekunuru. "Nicolás Guillén and Aimé Césaire: A 'Universalist' Approach to the Poetics of Africanness in Latin America and the Caribbean, 1929-1961," Washington, St. Louis, 1981.

739. Kutzinski, Vera Magret. "From American Literature to New World Writing: Myth and History in William Carlos Williams, Jay Wright, and Nicols Guillén," Yale, 1985.

740. Liddell, Janice Lee. "The Whip's Corolla: Myth and Politics in the Literature of the Black Diaspora: Aimé Césaire, Nicolás Guillén, Langston Hughes," Michigan, 1978.

741. Lowery, Dellita Martin. "Selected Poems of Nicolás Guillén and Langston Hughes: Their Use of Afro-Western Folk Music Genres." Ohio State, 1975.

742. Márquez, Robert. "Cuban Color: The Poetry of Nicols Guillén," Harvard, 1975.

743. Rogachevsky, Jorge Reubén. "Nicols Guillén and Herberto Padílla: The Revolutionary and the Romántic." SUNY, Buffalo, 1987.

744. Smart, Ian Isidore. "The Creative Dialogue in the Poetry of Nicolás Guillén: Europe and Africa," California, Los Angeles, 1975.

745. White, Clement A. "Myth and Verity in the Poetry of Nicolás Guillén: Confrontation, Crisis, Identification," Brown, 1987.

746. White, Florence E. "*Poesía Negra* in the Works of Jorge de Lima, Nicolás Guillén, and Jacques Roumain, 1927-1947," Wisconsin, 1952.

Manzano, Juan Francisco
See No. 748

Ortiz, Fernando
See Nos. 660, 732.

Suárez y Romero, Anselmo

747. Meson, Danusia Leah. 'Historia y Ficción en *Francisco*, Novela Antiesclavista Cubana del Siglo XIX," Maryland, 1987.

748. Netchinsky, Jill Ann. "Engendering a Cuban Literature: Nineteenth- century Antislavery Narrative (Manzano, Suárez y Romero, Gómez de Avellaneda, A. Zarmbrana)" Yale, 1986.

Zambrana, A.

See No. 748.

MUSIC AND DANCE

749. Asche, Charles Byron. "Cuban Folklore Traditions and Twentieth-Century Idioms in the Piano Works of Amadeo Roldn and Alejandro García Caturla," Texas, 1983.

750. Bissell, Sally Joan. "Manuel Areu and the Nineteenth-Century Zarzuela in Mexico and Cuba," Iowa, 1987.

751. Cornelius, Steven Harry. "The Convergence of Power: An Investigation into the Music Liturgy of Santería in New York City," California, Los Angeles, 1989.

752. Griffin, Robert James. Teaching Hispanic Folk Music as a Means to Cross-Cultural Understanding," Ohio State, 1973.

753. Jacobson, Gloria Castel. "The Life and Music of Ernesto Lecuona," Florida, 1982.

754. Mikowsky, Solomon Gadles. "The Nineteenth-Century Cuban *Danza* and Its Composers with Particular Attention to Ignacio Cervantes (1847-1905)," Columbia, 1973.

755. Rubin, Libby Antarsh. "Gottschalk in Cuba," Columbia, 1974.

756. Simó, Rita. "Stylistic Analysis of Piano Music of Latin America Since 1930," Boston University, 1975 [Ernesto Lecuona].

757. Yedra, Velia. "Julián Orbón: Biography and Analytical Study of *Tocata for Piano* and *Partitias No. 1 for Harpsichord*," University of Miami, 1986.

See also Nos. 792, 883, 893.

PSYCHOLOGY

General

758. Warren, Jerry. "Communal Therapy – Psychological and Social Integration for Those Labeled Schizophrenic," The Union for Experimenting Colleges and Universities, 1985 [Havana].

Psychology of Cubans in the United States

759. Azan, Alex Armando. "The MMPI Version Hispana: A Standardization and Cross-Cultural Personality Study With a Population of Cuban Refugees," Minnesota, 1989.

760. Bowen, Gladys Drummond. "Presenting Symptoms of Children and Adolescents at a Psychiatric Clinic: A Comparative Study of the Reported Symptoms of Black American, Cuban and White American Children," Florida State, 1981.

761. Casero, Enrique F. "The Attitudes of Cuban Americans Toward Seeking Psychotherapy," California School of Professional Psychology, Berkeley, 1982.

762. Estrada, Alejandrina Onelia. "The Children of Peter Pan: A Retrospective Study of the Migration of Unaccompanied Cuban Minors," The Wright Institute, 1988.

763. Fernández, Rose Mary. "An Empirical Test of the Minority Identity Development with Cuban Americans," Teachers College, Columbia, 1988.

764. Ghersi, Maria Zeralda. "Correlation Between Beck's Depression Inventory and Rotter's Locus of Control Questionnaire in a Hispanic Outpatient Population," Miami Institute of Psychology of the Caribbean Center for Advanced Studies, 1988.

765. González Reigosa, Fernando. "The Anxiety-Arousing Effect of Taboo Words in Bilinguals," Florida State, 1972.

766. Hernández, Cibeles. "Acculturation of Cuban Mothers and Children's Adjustment," Hofstra, 1982.

767. Llenin, Mercedes. "Correlation Between Suicidal Ideations and Self-Esteem in an Anglo-American and Cuban-American Population," Miami Institute of Psychology of the Caribbean Center for Advanced Studies, 1989.

768. Martínez Pons, Manuel. "The Relationship Between Family-Environmental Processes and Academic Achievement Among Three Hispanic Groups in the United States," CUNY, 1988.

769. Nazario Velasco, Edna. "Expectations, Self-Esteem, and Childhood Recollections of Inner City Hispanic Mothers of Low Birth-Weight Infants," CUNY, 1987.

770. Pando, José Ramón. "Appraisal of Various Clinical Scales of the Spanish Version of the Mini-Mult with Spanish Americans," Adelphi, 1974.

771. Pérez Ginart, David. "A Manual for the Psycho-Educational Assessment of Cuban Refugee Children," Rutgers, 1983 [Mariel Refugees].

772. Prado, Haydée. "Development of the Self-Concept in Anglo-American, Cuban-American and Cuban Children," Nova, 1983.

773. Rivera Sinclair, Elsa. "Cuban Latin Americans: Psychosocial Correlates of Cultural Adjustment," Maryland, 1988.

774. Rodríguez, Luis Juan. "Psychological Stress-Related Symptoms in a Tri-Ethnic Female Population," Miami

Institute of Psychology of the Caribbean Center for Advanced Studies, 1990.

775. Rodríguez Nogues, Lourdes. "Psychological Effects of Premature Separation from Parents in Cuban Refugee Girls: A Retrospective Study," Boston University, 1983.

776. Szapocznik, José. "Role Conflict in Cuban Mothers," University of Miami, 1977.

777. Tacher, Roberto David. "Traditional vs. Culturally Sensitive Family Therapy Sessions: A Comparison of Ratings by Cuban Immigrants," Texas, 1987 [Miami].

778. Weiss, Ana Delia. "Conduct Disorder and Father-Son Relationship in Cuban Entrant Boys." Miami Institute of Psychology of the Caribbean Center for Advanced Studies, 1988.

See also Nos. 783, 787, 846, 857, 868, 871, 891.

PUBLIC HEALTH, MEDICINE AND NURSING

779. Abu-Saad, Huda. "Nursing: A World View," Florida, 1977.

780. Danielson, Roswell S. "Cuban Health Organization: History and Development," Pittsburgh, 1973.

781. Feinsilver, Julie Margot. "Symbolic Politics and Health Policy: Cuba as a 'World Medical Power'," Yale, 1989.

782. González Dobles, Daniel. "The Ideological Determinants of Mental Health Programs and Practices: The Case of Cuba," South Carolina, 1989.

783. Hanna, Norma Cowley. "Insulin Dependent Diabetic Mellitus in Cuban-American Youths: Psychosocial Factors Related to Metabolic Control," University of Miami, 1984.

784. Liebowitz, Michael Robert. "The Cuban Health Care System: A Study in the Evaluation of Health Care Systems," Yale, 1969.

785. Maurer, Kurt Richard. "The Epidemiology of Gallstone Disease in the Mexican-American, Cuban American and Puerto Rican Populations of the United States, 1982-84," Johns Hopkins, 1988.

786. Mosher, Steven Aker. "The Right to Health: A Comparative Study of the Health Care Systems of the United States, Sweden and Cuba," South Carolina, 1980.

787. Plazas, Blanca-Rosa de la Torre. "Cuban-Americans and Mental Health; Cultural Framework and Theoretical Bases of a Preventive Educational Model," Loyola, Chicago, 1983.

See also Nos. 844, 857, 868.

RELIGION AND RELIGIOUS HISTORY

788. Bryant, Glenn E. "History of Baptist Mission Work in Cuba," Central Baptist Theological Seminary, Kansas City, Kansas," 1954.

789. Delgado, Primitivo. "The History of Southern Baptist Missions in Cuba to 1945," Southern Baptist Theological Seminary, 1948.

790. Fahy, Joseph Augustine. "The Antislavery Thought of José Agustín Caballero, Juan José Díaz de Espada, and Félix Varela in Cuba, 1791-1823," Harvard, 1983.

791. Greer, Harold Edward Jr. "History of Southern Baptist Mission Work in Cuba, 1886-1916," Alabama, 1965.

792. McConnell, Harry G. "The Development of the Hymn Among Spanish-Speaking Evangelicals," Southern Baptist Theological Seminary, 1953.

793. Murphy, Joseph M. "Ritual Systems in Cuban Santería," Temple, 1981.

794. Reuter, Frank Theodore. "Church and State in the American Dependencies 1898-1904: A Study of Catholic

Opinion and the Formulation of Colonial Policy," Illinois, 1960.

795. Rosado, Caleb. "Sect and Party: Religion under Revolution in Cuba [a Study of the Seventh Day Adventist Church in Cuba as a Sect in Conflict with the Communist Party]," Northwestern, 1985.

796. Shephard, William Hendy. "An Exploration of the Effectiveness of Denominational Influence Upon Students of a Mission School in Cuba," Maryland, 1955.

See also Nos. 214, 437, 751, 890.

SCIENCE (BOTANY, ENTOMOLOGY, ETC.)

797. Arce, Gina. "A Study of Some Chlorophyceae from Cuban Soil," Vanderbilt, 1957.

798. Bates, Drell Marston. "The Butterflies of Cuba," Harvard, 1934.

799. Dougherty, Veronica Mary. "A Systematic Revision of the New World Ectrichodiinae (Hemiptera: Reduviidae)," Connecticut, 1980.

800. Ellis, Brooks Fleming. "Study of Discoidal Foraminifera from Cuba," New York, 1932.

801. Gerry, B. "Cuban Mosquitoes," Harvard, 1931.

802. Hatheway, William Howell. "Races of Maize in Cuba," Harvard, 1953.

803. Hedges, Stephen Blair. "Evolution and Biogeography of West Indian Frogs of the Genus *Eleutherodactylus*: Slow-Evolving Loci and the Major Groups," Maryland, 1988.

804. Johnson, Victor. "A Review of the Coniopterygidae of North America and Central America," Kentucky, 1977.

805. Pashley, David Neal. "A Distributional Analysis of the Warblers of the West Indies," Louisiana State, 1988.

806. Southall, Russell Melvin. "A Taxonomic Revision of Kalmia (Ericaceae)," North Carolina State, Raleigh, 1973.

807. Spellman, David Leonard. "A Revision of the Genus *Fischeria* (Asclepiadaceae)," Saint Louis, 1975.

SOCIOLOGY AND CULTURAL ANTHROPOLOGY

In Cuba

808. Booth, D.K. "Neighborhood Committees and Popular Courts in the Social Transformation of Cuba," Surrey, 1975.

809. Bunck, Julie Marie. "Culture Change in Postrevolutionary Cuba," Virginia, 1988.

810. Chang, Ching Chieh. "The Chinese in Latin America, a Preliminary Geographical Survey With Special Reference to Cuba and Jamaica," Maryland, 1956.

811. Collver, Orville Andrew. "Birth Rates in Latin America: New Estimates of Historical Trends and Fluctuations," California, Berkeley, 1964.

812. Díaz Briquets, Sergio. "Mortality in Cuba: Trends and Determinants, 1880-1971," Pennsylvania, 1977.

813. Edwardh, Carol Joann. "The Older Generation: An Ecological Study of Old Age in Havana," Syracuse, 1979.

814. Farber, Samuel. "Revolution and Social Structure in Cuba, 1933-1959," California, Berkeley, 1969.

815. Fitzgerald, Frank Thomas. "Politics and Social Structure in Revolutionary Cuba: From the Demise of the Old Middle Class to the Rise of the New Professionals," SUNY, Binghamton, 1985.

816. Hutchens, Rex Richard. "Women in Cuba: Education and Directed Culture Change," Arizona, 1984.

817. Landstreet, Barent French, Jr. "Cuban Population Issues in Historical and Comparative Perspective," Cornell, 1976.

818. Martínez Alier, V. "Marriage, Class, and Colour in Nineteenth-Century Cuba," Oxford, 1970.

819. Mulhare, Mirta de la Torre. "Sexual Ideology in Pre-Castro Cuba: A Cultural Analysis," Pittsburgh, 1969.

820. Naimi, M.T. "Toward a Theory of Postrevolutionary Social Change: A Six Nation Comparative Study," Washington State, 1985.

821. Parrilla Cruz, Carmen Eneida. "Coming into Being Among the Cuban Women," New School for Social Research, 1983.

822. Pettitt, Michael Anthony. "Social and Economic Change in the Community Around a Sugar Mill in Cuba," California, Berkeley, 1973.

See also Nos. 298, 424, 425, 884.

In the United States

General

823. Aguirre López, Beniono Emilio. "The Marital Stability of Cuban Immigrants: 1970," Ohio State, 1977.

824. Akulicz de Santiago, Anne Marie. "Residential Segregation of Spanish Origin Populations: A Study of Recent Trends in a Sample of U.S. Cities," Wisconsin, 1984.

825. ArgHelles, Maria de Lourdes R. "Cuban Political Refugees in the United States: A Study of Social Mobility and Authoritarianism," New York, 1970.

826. Canas Martínez, Jorge J. "The Cuban Immigrant of 1980: An Exploration of Psycho-social Issues in the Migration Experience Through the Topical Life History Method," Boston University, 1984.

827. Cintrón de Esteves, Carmen M. "A Comparison of Cultural Traditions Among Four Hispanic Groups in the United States," Texas Woman's, 1981.

828. Clark, Juan Marcial. "The Exodus from Revolutionary Cuba (1959-1974): A Sociological Analysis," Florida, 1975.

829. Cohen, Steven Martin. "Patterns of Interethnic Marriage and Friendship in the United States," Columbia, 1974.

830. Colmenero, José Antonio. "Issues and Problems of Cuban Identity and Acculturation," North Carolina, Greensboro, 1985.

831. Doby, Silvio Victor. "Common Law and Civil Law Interactions: Their Effect on Migrants within the Americas," Fordham, 1987.

832. Gallagher, Patrick Lee. "The Cuban Exile, A Socio-Political Analysis," St. Louis, 1974.

833. Gibboney, Joseph Dominic. "Stability and Change in Components of Parental Role Among Cuban Refugees," Catholic, 1967.

834. Massey, Douglas Steven. "Residential Segregation of Spanish Americans in United States Urbanized Areas," Princeton, 1978.

835. Namazi, Kevan H. "Assimilation and Need Assessment Among Mexican, Cuban, and Middle Eastern Immigrants: A Multivariate Analysis," Akron, 1984.

836. Ortíz, Karol Roccena. "Accounts of Desperate Times: Six Cuban Refugee Life Histories," California, Irvine, 1983.

837. Pedraza Bailey, Sílvia. "Political and Economic Migrants in America: Cubans and Mexicans," Chicago, 1980.

838. Stevenson, James Milton. "Cuban-Americans: New Urban Class," Wayne State, 1973.

839. Verdugo, Naomi Turner. "Earnings Differences Among Black, White and Hispanic Males and Females: The Impact of Overeducation, Undereducation and Discrimination," Southern California, 1985.

See also Nos. 181, 427, 428, 432, 771, 772, 821.

California

840. Gil, Vincent Edward. "The Personal Adjustment and Acculturation of Cuban Immigrants in Los Angeles," California, Los Angeles, 1976.

Florida

841. Bryant, Carol Anne. "The Impact of Kin, Friend and Neighbor Networks of Infantile Obesity," Kentucky, 1978 [Dade County].

842. Dowd, Donald Jerome. "A Comparative Study of Attitudes, Goals, and Values Between Negro American, White American, and Cuban Refugee Groups in a Large Southern City," Florida, 1966 [Miami].

843. Erwin, Nancy Elizabeth. "The Importance of Neighborhoods for Cuban Americans in Greater Miami," Florida, 1984.

844. García Cabrera, Angelita. "The Hispanic Veterans of the Armed Services and the Veterans Administration," Brandeis, 1978.

845. Hernández Peck, María Cristina. "Frail Elderly Cubans: Decision Making for Their Long-Term Care," Denver, 1980 [Miami].

846. Lee, Linda Mobley. "Family, Dynamics and Role Strain in Hispanic and Non-Hispanic Married, Employed Women with Preschool Children," University of Miami, 1987.

847. Morgan, Ivette de Arteaga. "Factors Affecting Acculturation of Cuban Refugee Students in Miami," University of Miami, 1977.

848. Redondo Carbonell, José Pedro. "Migration as a Critical Transition: A Comparison of the Expereinces of Puerto Rican and Cuban Adolescents," Clark, 1983 [Miami].

849. Richmond, Marie La Liberté. "Immigrant Adaptation and Family Structure Among Cubans in Miami, Florida," Florida State, 1973.

850. Thompson, Sylvia Ann. "Community Leadership in Greater Miami, Florida: What Role for Blacks and Cuban-Americans?" Southern Illinois, 1985.

See No. 430.

Illinois

851. Durán, Daniel Flores. "Latino Communication Patterns: An Investigation of Media Use and Organizational Activity Among Mexican, Cuban, and Puerto Rican Residents of Chicago," Wisconsin, 1977.

852. Fox, Geoffrey Edmund. "Working-Class Emigrés from Cuba. A Study of Counter-Revolutionary Consciousness," Northwestern, 1975 [Chicago].

See also Nos. 429, 431.

Louisiana

853. Carballo, Manuel. "A Socio-Psychological Study of Acculturation/Assimilation: Cubans in New Orleans, Tulane, 1970.

854. Williamson, David. "Cognitive Complexity and Adaptation to Socio-Cultural Change: The Case of the Cuban Refugees in New Orleans," Tulane, 1973.

Massachusetts

855. Sanders, Joseph Paul. "The Impact of Migration and Other Variables on the Physical and Mental Health of Hispanic Migrants to Boston," Boston College, 1986.

Michigan

856. Mesa, José Luis. "Intra-Urban Residential Mobility and Ethnicity: Cuban-Americans in Lansing, Michigan," Michigan State, 1978.

New Jersey

857. Gómez, Manuel Rafael. "Biculturalism and Subjective Mental Health Among Cuban Americans," New York, 1987.

858. Prieto, Yolanda, "Reinterpreting an Immigration Success Story: Cuban Women, Work, and Change in a New Jersey Community," Rutgers, 1984.

859. Rogg, Eleanor Hertha. "The Occupational Adjustment of Cuban Refugees in the West New York, New Jersey Area," Fordham, 1970.

See also No. 861.

Greater New York

860. Brandon, George Edward. "The Dead Sell Memories: An Anthropological Study of Santería in New York City," Rutgers, 1983.

861. Brown, David Hilary. "Garden in the Machine: Afro-Cuban Sacred Art and Performance in Urban New Jersey and New York," Yale, 1989.

862. Gregory, Steven. "Santería in New York City: A Study in Cultural Resistance," New School for Social Research, 1986.

863. Pasquali, Elaine Anne. "Assimilation and Acculturation of Cubans on Long Island," SUNY, Stony Brook, 1982.

See also No. 426.

Washington, D.C.

864. Boone, Margaret Stanley. "Cubans in City Context: The Washington Case," Ohio State, 1977.

San Juan, Puerto Rico

865. Duany, Jorge Luis. "The Cubans of Puerto Rico: Socioeconomic Adaptation in a Caribbean City," California, Berkeley, 1985.

SPORT AND RECREATION

866. Pettavino, Paula Jean. "The Politics of Sport Under Communism: A Comparative Study of Competitive Athletics in the Soviet Union and Cuba," Notre Dame, 1982.

88 JESSE J. DOSSICK

867. Regalado, Samuel. "The Special Hunger: Latin Americans in American Professional Baseball, 1871-1970." Washington State, 1987.

URBAN AND REGIONAL PLANNING

868. Rivas, Priscilla. "Primary Health Care and Planning in Cuba and Costa Rica," Cornell, 1988.

See also No. 37.

ADDENDA

869. Gosser, Mary Ann. "'Conversación en la Catedral' and 'Cobra'" (per) versions of French Narratives. Yale, 1990.

870. Hanson, Gail. "Summer Welles and the American System: The United States in the Caribbean, 1920-1940," SUNY, Stony Brook, 1990.

871. Kosarchyn, Chrystyna. "An Investigation of the Health Needs of Hispanic Elementary School Children as Perceived by School Nurses." Toledo, 1990.

872. Lugo-Ortiz, Agnes Ivelisse. "Identidades Inauguradas: Biografía y Nacionalidad en Cuba, 1860-1898." Princeton, 1990.

873. Mayta, Fabin Esteban. "The Relationship of Mathematics Computation with Concrete Reasoning Ability, Math Attitudes and Four Demographic Variables of English and Spanish-Speaking Incarcerated Adult Males." University of Miami, 1990.

874. McGovern, Eileen Marie. "From Varela to Martí: Four Nineteenth Century Cuban Emigré Newspapers." Temple, 1990.

875. Nuri, Maqsud Ulhasan. "Cuban Policy in Africa: The Limits of the Proxy Model." South Carolina, 1990.

876. Pérez Marín, Carmen Ivette. "El Poema en Prosa en Hispanoamérica. Harvard, 1990.

877. Rice, Donald Everett. "The Rhetorical Uses of the Authorizing Figure: Fidel Castro and José Martí. Iowa, 1990.

878. Sand. Louise. "The Role of Federico Hanssen and Rodolfo Lenz in the Intellectual Life of Chile." North Carolina, 1958.

879. Torres Pou, Juan. "El E(x) terno Femenino: Estereotipos Femeninos en la Literatura Hispanoamericana del Siglo XIX." Rutgers, 1990.

880. Ayala, César J. "Industrial Oligopoly and Vertical Integration: the Origins of the American Sugar Kingdom in the Caribbean, 1881-1921, " SUNY, Binghampton, 1991.

881. Barquet, Jesús José. "El Grupo Orígenes y la Eticidad Cubana; Recuento de un Proceso," Tulane, 1990.

882. Chirol, Marie-Magdaleine. "Ruines et imaginaire de la ruine dans le roman du 20 éme siècle: Proust, Carpentier, Céla, Duras, Nyssen, Jean," Maryland, 1991.

883. Daniel, Yvonne La Vérne Payne. "Ethnography of Rumba: Dance and Social Change in Contemporary Cuba," California, Berkeley, 1989.

884. Funkhouser, Edward. "Essays on International Migration: The Sender Country and Migrant Perspectives," Harvard, 1990.

885. Gibian, Jill Lisa. "Three Ways of Rewriting a Text: Parody, Translation, and Criticism. The Latin American Model: A Sociocultural Analysis," SUNY, Binghamton, 1991. [Guillermo Cabrera Infante - Tres Tristes].

886. Heller, Ben Amers. "A Hermeneutic Approach to José Lezama Lima's Poetry of Assimilation," Washington, St. Louis, 1991.

887. Karim, Manjur. "World System and Export Economics: A Comparative Analysis of Cuba and Taiwan," Kansas State, 1990.

888. Kwon, Hyuk - Bum. "The Politics of Transition to Socialism in Cuba and North Korea," Massachusetts, 1990.

889. Mc Bride, William Michael. "The Rise and Fall of a Strategic Technology: The American Battleship from Santiago Bay to Pearl Harbor, 1898-1941," Johns Hopkins, 1990.

890. Morales, Beatriz. "Afro-Cuban Religious Transformation: A Comparative Study of Lucumí Religion and the Tradition of Spirit Belief," CUNY, 1990.

891. Owen, Roger Griffith. "Ego Identity Status Distributions of Anglo and Cuban-American College Males and Tests of Status-By-Culture Interaction on Measures of Psychological Development and Self-Esteem," University of Miami, 1984.

892. Piedra, Armando J. "La Revista Cubana 'Origenes' (1944-1956): Portavoz Generacional," Florida, 1977.

893. Robbins, James Lawrence. "Making Popular Music in Cuba: A Study of the Cuban Institutions of Musical Production and the Musical Life of Santiago de Cuba," Illinois, 1990.

894. Sandrol, Paul Charles. "Castro's Cuba and Stroessner's Paraguay: A Comparison of the Totalitarian/Authoritarian Taxonomy," Arizona , 1990.

895. Tremayne, Russell Mark. "Delusions and Reality: The Evolution of Frank Church's Ideas on U.S.-Latin American Policy, 1956-1980," Washington, Seattle, 1990.

896. Utting, P. "The Political Economy of Economic and Food Policy Reform in Third World Socialist Countries, Essex, 1990.

897. Figueras, Carlos. "Desdoblamiento E. Identitad: La Cuestión del Sujeto y el Desvanecimiento de Absolutos en la Narrativa Hispanoamericana Contempornea: Ouetti, Cortázar, Sarduy," Texas, 1991.

898. Horno Delgado, Asunción Victoria. "Liquidificación, Marginalidad y Misticismo: Construcción del Imaginario en la Lírica de Dulce María Loynaz." Massachusetts, 1991.

899. Reed, Roger Alan. "The Evolution of Cultural Policy in Cuba: From the Fall of Batista to the Padilla Case,: Université de Genève, Switzerland, 1989.

900. Stein, Susan Isabel. "Reading between the Lie: Self-Fictionalization as Narrative Strategy in "La Voregine', 'El Trivel', and 'Los Pasos Perdidos'," California, Irvine, 1991.

INDEX TO NAMES IN TITLES OF DISSERTATIONS

INDEX OF AUTHORS

A

Alba, Elio, 673
Alexander, Roberta May, 530
Allabar, Anton Laurence, 424
Allen, David Harding, Jr., 634
Allison, Graham Tillett, Jr., 364
Alonso, Juan Manuel, 531
Alonso, Luis Ricardo, 635
Alonso, Miriam G., 83
Alvarado, Ela E., 500
Alvarez, Nicols Emilio, 628
Alvarez, Rolando, 85
Amor, Sister Rosa Teresa, 492
Andino, Alberto, 636
Angulo, Mauria-Elena, 532
Arce, Gina, 797
Argu.lles, Maria de Lourdes R., 825
Arnes, Jonathan F., 86
Arnov, Venice Beaulieu, 117
Arrom, José Juan, 15
Artalejo, Lucrecía, 625
Asche, Charles Byron, 749
Assardo, Maurice Roberto, 533
Assetto, Valerie J., 265
Auxier, George Washington, 353
Ayala, César J., 880
Azan, Alex Armando, 759
Azicri, Max, 266
Azize, Yamila, 494

B

Badillo, David A., 247
Bailey, Jennifer Leigh, 338
Baird, Keith Ethelbert, 434
Baker, Armand Fred, 534
Baker, Thomas Hart, Jr., 187
Ballon - A, José Carlos, 637
Baloyra, Enrique Antonio, 248
Barilleaux, Ryan John, 361
Barnes, Arthur M., 204
Barnett, Curtis L.E., 660
Barquet, Jesús José, 881
Barradás, Efrain, 495

Barreda, Pedro Manuel, 715
Barroso, Juan, VIII, 535
Bass, Bernice Marie, 97
Bates, Drell Marston, 798
Bates, Thomas Hobson, 384
Batie, Robert Carlyle, 43
Baxter, J.R., 536
Beaupied, Aida María, 698
Belcher, Jack Benjamin, 188
Beltrán Vocal, Maria Antonia, 537
Bender, Lynn Darrell, 339
Benjamin, Charles Michael, 365
Benjamin, Jules Robert, 324
Benz, Stephen Lee, 455
Bernardo, Roberto Medina, 37
Bernstein, Richard Eric, 1
Berry, Lee Roy, Jr., 311
Bertot, Lillian D., 699
Biandudi, Joncker K. Ibn, 299
Bissell, Sally Joan, 750
Bjarkman, Peter Christian, 436
Blasier, Stewart Cole, 407
Bonachea, Rolando E., 340
Boone, Margaret Stanley, 864
Booth, D.K., 808
Borgman, Ruth Elizabeth, 616
Bornstein, Miriam Mijalina, 691
Bortolussi, Marisa, 477
Borunda, Mario Rene, 118
Bostdorff, Denise Marie, 366
Boughton, George John, 408
Boulware Miller, Patricia Kay, 728
Bowen, Gladys Drummond, 760
Boyd, Antonio Olliz, 729
Boydston, Jo Ann Harrison, 456
Boyer, Harold, 393
Boynton, Maryanna Craig, 312
Bradford, Richard Headlee, 161
Brainard, Clarice H., 87
Brandon, George Edward, 860
Bresnahan, Roger James, 478
Brodermann, Ramón E., 638
Brotherson, Festus, Jr., 300

D

E

Edelstein, Joel Calvin, 301
Edwardh, Carol Joann, 813
Edwards, Flora Mancuso, 17
Einaudi, Luigi Roberto, 272
Elie, Gerri Moore, 124
Elliott, Norma Jean, 18
Ellis, Brooks Fleming, 800
Ellmore, Winant Stubbs, 191
Engel, James Franklin, 404
Erisman, H. Michael, 249
Erwin, Nancy Elizabeth, 843
Estrada, Alejandrina Onelia, 762
Ettinger, Amos A., 165
Evans, Bette Novit, 273

F

Fagon, Donald O'Connor, 423
Fahy, Joseph Augustine, 790
Fails, Willis Clark, 438
Falk, Pamela S., 274
Farber, Samuel, 814
Fariñas, Lucila, 675
Farrell, Joseph Richard, 737
Fast, J.S., 47
Favi, Jeane D., 460
Feal, Rosemary Geisdorfer, 514
Febles, Jorge Manuel, 612
Feinsilver, Julie Margot, 781
Ferguson, Theresa P., 515
Fermoselle López, Rafael, 235
Fernández, Damian J., 418
Fernández, Lilia, 713
Fernández, Luis Francisco, 620
Fernández, Ricardo R., 551
Fernández, Roberto G., 490
Fernández, Rose Mary, 763
Fernández Fernández, Ramiro, 672
Fernández Rubio, Ramón, 552
Fernández Valledor, Roberto, 461
Fernández Vásquez, Antonio A., 491
Figueras, Carlos, 899

H

Hopf, Carroll Henry, 314
Horno Delgado, Asunción Victoria, 898
Howard, Philip Anthony, 168
Hulse, Frederick Seymour, 8
Hunter, John M., 51
Hutchens, Rex Richard, 816
Hynes, Mary Ellen, 110

I

Iduart, Andrés, 642
Iglesias, Alex, 279
Incledon, John Scott, 668
Inglis, Gordon Douglas, 155
Isern, Margarita, 125

J

Jackman, Francis V., 330
Jackson, Sandra Carter, 74
Jackson, Shirley Mae, 725
Jacobs, C.C., 193
Jacobs, Roderick Arnold, 441
Jacobson, Gloria Castel, 753
Jaguaribe de Mattos, Beatriz, 561
Janney, Frank Fay, 562
Jensen, Larry Russell, 156
Jervis, David T., 344
Jiménez Sánchez, Reynaldo Luis, 518
Johnson, Maribel Dicker, 466
Johnson, Phillip, 467
Johnson, Victor, 804
Jones, D.B., 56
Jones, Julie, 563
Jones, Lewis P., 468
Jones, Roger Eugene, 280
Judicini, Joseph Victor, 606
Judson, Charles Frederick, 306

K

Kanowski, P.J., 2
Kapcia, A.M., 469
Kapschutschenko, Ludmila, 564

L

Layson, Walter Wells, 370
Lazcano, Antonio María, 607
Leahy, Margaret Ellen, 282
Leard, Robert B., 173
Leblanc, Lawrence Joseph, 309
Ledesma de los Reyes, Pedro Pablo, 511
Lee, Linda Mobley, 846
Léger, Love O., 398
Leogrande, William Mark, 283
Leon, Charles F., 60
Leroy, Jean Landri, 321
Lester, Margaret Nancy, 568
Liddell, Janice Lee, 740
Liebowitz, Michael Robert, 784
Llenin, Mercedes, 767
Lockmiller, David A., 237
López, Ana M., 13
López Ramírez, Tomás, 663
Lord, Carmen Betancourt, 111
Losman, Donald Lee, 40
Lowery, Dellita Martin, 741
Lugo-Ortiz, Agnes Ivelisse, 872
Luis, William, 615
Lumsden, Charles Ian, 303
Lutjens, Sheryl Lea, 284
Lutz, Robyn Rothrock, 703

M

Mac Donald, Marguerite Goodrich, 443
Mac Master, Richard Kerwin, 174
Mack, Mary T., 101
Magnarelli, Sharon Dishaw, 515
Mandelbaum, Ann, 569
Marina, Dorita Roca, 112
Maris, Gary Leroy, 322
Markel, Robert Thomas, 386
Marqués, Sarah, 626
Márquez, Enrique, 704
Márquez, Robert, 742
Martí, Jorge Luis, 630
Martin, Claire Emilie, 570
Martínez Alier, V., 818

N

O

P

Q

R

Rogg, Eleanor Hertha, 859
Rojas Paiewonsky, Lourdes, 586
Rosado, Caleb, 795
Rose, Gregory Frank, 290
Rosell, Raúl Gonzalo, 242
Rosello, Aurora Julia, 694
Rosenbaum, H. Jon, 401
Rosenberg, Emile, 93
Ross, Bernard Harvey, 377
Rossell, Ana E., 115
Rostagno, Irene, 474
Rotker, Susana R., 651
Rowe, Joseph Milton, Jr., 243
Rozencvaig, Perla, 503
Rubén, Francisco, 689
Rubin, Libby Antarsh, 755
Ruff, Thomas Peter, 221
Ruffin, Patricia, 316
Russell, Charles Alvin, 291
Ryan, Jeffrey John, 263
Rys, John Frank, 253

S

Sadler, Louis Ray, 254
Salazar, Carol Lacy, 587
Salces, Luis Mario, 429
Saldivar, José David, 588
Salvucci, Linda Kerrigan, 160
Sánchez, Marta Ester, 589
Sánchez, Napoléon Neptali, 590
Sánchez, Nicolás, 57
Sánchez-Eppler, Benigno, 497
Sand, Louise, 878
Sanders, Joseph Paul, 855
Sandman, Joshua Harry, 378
Santiago, Bessie Norma, 450
Santiago, Emelina, 131
Santos, Richard, 73
Scheina, Robert Lewis, 308
Schellings, William John, 222
Schreiber, Anna Panayotou, 310
Schulman, Ivan Albert, 652

For Product Safety Concerns and Information please contact our EU
representative GPSR@taylorandfrancis.com
Taylor & Francis Verlag GmbH, Kaufingerstraße 24, 80331 München, Germany

* 9 7 8 0 9 3 5 5 0 1 4 9 0 *